The Battle of Mill Springs Kentucky

The Battle of Mill Springs Kentucky

Stuart W. Sanders

The History Press

Published by The History Press
Charleston, SC 29403
www.historypress.net

First published 2013

Manufactured in the United States

ISBN 978.1.60949.829.0

Library of Congress CIP data applied for.

Notice: The information in this book is true and complete to the best of our knowledge. It is offered without guarantee on the part of the author or The History Press. The author and The History Press disclaim all liability in connection with the use of this book.

Contents

Acknowledgements

This tale begins with a ghost story. Not an exciting one, I'm afraid, or a terrifying one. It is, nonetheless, a ghost story, and one that got me interested in the Battle of Mill Springs.

Several years ago, I toured the Mill Springs battlefield as part of a heritage tourism event that I helped organize. When the tour began, I stood behind the group, near the spot where Confederate General Felix Zollicoffer had been killed. As the guide talked about the campaign, something gently squeezed the back of my arm. I turned around, expecting to see a friend who had helped organize the tour. No one was behind me. No one was near me. Surprised, I turned around twice in a circle, trying to see who it could have been. No one was there.

I have no explanation. For the sake of argument, let us simply say that it was a mild pull from the past. It was neither jarring nor frightening. Instead, it was a "pay attention to me" or an "I'm here" moment. With this book, I hope that I have paid adequate attention.

While that surprising event got me interested in the subject, many people have helped along the way.

First, many thanks go to several research repositories and their staffs, including the Kentucky Historical Society, Roger Stapleton and the Kentucky Heritage Council, Jim Holmberg and the archivists at the Filson Historical Society, the Indiana Historical Society and Karyn Branham, former director of the Mill Springs Battlefield Association.

Mark D. Jaeger was extremely generous and provided me with several crucial sources about the 10th Indiana Infantry Regiment. Many of these sources were vital for this book, and I greatly appreciate his willingness to help.

A thank-you to those who supplied images, including the Library of Congress; Jennifer Duplaga and Charley Pallos at the Kentucky Historical Society; Jim Campi and Mary Koik at the Civil War Trust; Joseph E. Brent and Maria Brent with Mudpuppy and Waterdog, Inc.; and Bob Glass of Centre College.

Thanks to Bill Neikirk, former president of the Mill Springs Battlefield Association. I could not have written this book without his leading me on an extensive tour of the battlefield. Bill's knowledge of the archaeological evidence and his comprehension of the terrain were vital in formulating my understanding of the battle. Bill also read the manuscript and made some very helpful suggestions.

I am grateful for supportive friends Erik Drake and Mignon Brousseau, Steve and Amy Isola, John and Andrea Mesplay and their families. Additional thanks go to Brian Grimmer, Gary Neighbors, Cindy Neighbors, Brian Neighbors, Heather Neighbors, Mark Read, Harv Smith, Robert H. Williams and W. L. Wilson. Much appreciation for my brother, Wallace Sanders, and my sister-in-law, Catherine Edwards Sanders.

Many thanks to my editor, Banks Smither, and the staff of The History Press. Working with The History Press on my first book, *Perryville Under Fire: The Aftermath of Kentucky's Largest Battle*, was a great experience, and this project has been equally fulfilling.

I also thank my colleague Tim Talbott, who kindly read the manuscript and made important suggestions.

I appreciate the encouragement of my friend, colleague and fellow carpooler Don Rightmyer. Don and his wife, Bonnie, both read the manuscript, and I appreciate their comments.

My parents were extremely supportive and were very helpful editors. My father, Dr. I. Taylor Sanders II, taught history at Washington and Lee University for forty-two years, while my mother, Barbara Sanders, is a former English teacher. I am appreciative of their editorial skills but more thankful to have them as parents.

The best part of writing this book is that it gave me the opportunity to tromp around the battlefield with my wife, Jenny, and our three wonderful children: John, Anne and Elizabeth. Although my youngest worried about nonexistent bears in the woods, she had her two older siblings to protect her. We saw no bears, but it was a day that I will always remember. Therefore, I dedicate this book to them, with much love.

Introduction

The three boys walked toward the battlefield, their picks and shovels slung over slender shoulders. One of them, barely ten years old, was pulled to the recent scene of fighting by his older brothers. As the trio neared the battleground, they passed the abandoned accoutrements of war; muskets, bayonets, coats and cartridge boxes lay scattered, thrown away by fleeing soldiers. The boys probably knew little about the fight that had happened near their homes. As they watched wagons full of wounded soldiers rumble away, however, they might have spoken of the Rebel general Zollicoffer, who was shot down before his solders fled to the swollen Cumberland River.

Youthful chatter ended when they reached the field. "After the battle nobody knew what to do," one later wrote.

> *The bodies were all covered up with ice and everyone was running around crying. Father hitched the mules up to a dirt scoop and dug three long trenches to place the bodies in. The bodies were frozen to the ground and we had to take shovels and pry them from the ground... We stacked the bodies in the wagon like firewood, legs, hands, and arms were in odd postures and some bodies did not have all of their parts. The bodies were placed in the trenches and covered.*[1]

While these soldiers were the immediate casualties from the Battle of Mill Springs, Kentucky, others contended with longer-lasting consequences. When the fighting raged, Confederate officer Bailie Peyton shot Union lieutenant

Tenbroeck Strout near the spine. An operation was deemed too dangerous, so the bullet remained in Strout's back. In 1880, more than eighteen years after the battle, Strout reportedly died of lead poisoning, making him a final casualty of the Battle of Mill Springs. Peyton, who was shot in the face and killed immediately after he wounded Strout, lived on in his family's memory. His father's sword, which Peyton wore during the fight, eventually carried one man's hope for sectional reconciliation. In 1907, M.C. Tuttle, whose family had kept the sword since the battle, wrote to Bailie's brother. Since the war was long over, Tuttle wanted to return the sword to the family. "I sincerely trust that it may never be unsheathed again unless in defense of all the stars and stripes," Tuttle wrote.

The three boys who helped their father inter the Rebel dead were never psychologically reconciled. In later years, the brothers reputedly suffered mental trauma, and one—who killed one of the others—supposedly died in an insane asylum. These were the forgotten casualties of Mill Springs. As Confederate veteran Bennett Young penned, the fight was one "full of pathos and tragedy."[2]

Although small when compared to later battles, Mill Springs was an action of great consequence. Fought in the mud, fog and rain on January 19, 1862, it was a turning point in the American Civil War. As the first major Union victory since the Federal disaster at the Battle of Bull Run, fought in Manassas, Virginia, six months earlier, Mill Springs was widely celebrated across the North. The battle, and the death of Confederate General Felix Zollicoffer, garnered broad media attention and pushed Union officers Speed Fry and George Thomas into the national spotlight. Ultimately, the Federal victory at Mill Springs snapped the right flank of a Confederate defensive line that spanned across southern Kentucky. The collapse of this line ended the Southerners' first attempt to hold Kentucky for the Confederacy, left the Bluegrass State in Union hands and opened large swaths of Tennessee for Federal invasion. Fought four months after Kentucky officially ended the state's neutrality, the Northern victory undoubtedly pushed some undecided Kentuckians into the Union camp.

The armies were mostly composed of inexperienced and poorly drilled soldiers. When the fighting raged in the hilly, wooded terrain in abominable weather, unit cohesion fragmented. Portions of regiments became mixed with other units. Therefore, individual soldiers' experiences sometimes differed, even when they fought in the same regiment. The terrain, the troops' inability to see friendly regiments, the fog, smoke, rain and the lack of unit cohesion led to contradictory battle accounts, claims of falsified reports, accusations of drunkenness and courts-martial. In brief, Mill Springs was a fight marked by chaos. The shooting of Zollicoffer after he accidentally wandered into Union lines was emblematic of this confusion.

Sadly, and despite the fight's significance, today the battle is more commonly recognized as a trivia question. It has been called by more names than perhaps any other Civil War battle. It has been dubbed Mill Springs, Fishing Creek, Logan's Crossroads, Beech Grove, Cliff Creek, Webb's Crossroads, the Battle of Somerset, the Battle of Old Fields, the Battle of Logan's Fields, the Battle of the Cumberland and more.[3]

Squabbles about what to call the action started as soon as the fighting ended. Six days after the engagement, the *Chicago Tribune* noted that "there is as yet no uniformity in giving a name to the battle." As early as February 19, 1862, newspapers poked fun at the number of names. The *Goodhue Volunteer* of Red Wing, Minnesota, wrote, "We propose as far as the rebels are concerned, they compromise the matter by calling it the 'Big Lick.'" As late as 1910, editors of *Confederate Veteran* magazine pondered the issue, deciding that "Mill Springs" did not work because the settlement of that name was "miles away and across the Cumberland River" from the battlefield. Furthermore, Fishing Creek was "miles distant in the opposite direction." The editors decided that Logan's Crossroads or Nancy, the town just north of the battlefield, were more viable options. In the end, however, the editors remained perplexed, asking, "Who can suggest relief from the unfortunate dilemma? There ought to be a fixed single name for it." Although this issue has lessened over time, in this book I refer to the action as the Battle of Mill Springs, which is today the most commonly used name. It is also the one embraced by the organization working to preserve the field, the Mill Springs Battlefield Association.[4]

Although Mill Springs was overshadowed by later engagements, those who survived the fight understood its significance. So, too, did some of the highest officeholders in the Union. Shortly after the battle, U.S. Senator John J. Crittenden, whose efforts at compromise had failed to avert the Civil War, offered a petition to Congress. Crittenden, a Kentucky Unionist whose son had led the Confederate army at Mill Springs, called for George Washington's Farewell Address to be read in Congress on February 22, 1862. Another congressman soon added an amendment to the petition, calling for a public reading of the Declaration of Independence. Importantly, he also called for a reading of Secretary of War Edwin Stanton's congratulatory order sent to Union General George H. Thomas after Thomas's victory at Mill Springs. Congress wanted the victory recognized on the national stage. In addition, veterans of the battle—and proud members of the U.S. Congress—believed that the Civil War would end shortly after Mill Springs. Instead, the episode touched off a chain of events that spiraled Confederate hopes west of the Appalachian Mountains downward and showed the divided nation that the Civil War would be a long struggle.[5]

Chapter 1

At the end of September 1861, Ellen Wallace of Hopkinsville, Kentucky, wrote, "War and nothing but war is the order of the day." The Bluegrass State's short-lived neutrality had just ended, and Union and Confederate troops swarmed into the commonwealth. For those familiar with Kentucky's political fathers, including Henry Clay and John J. Crittenden, neutrality seemed to be a sensible stance. In the past, Kentucky leaders had forged compromises to avert sectional conflict. After the 1860 election of Kentucky-born Republican president Abraham Lincoln, however, words of conciliation failed. Southern states seceded, civil war erupted and, in May 1861, Kentucky officially declared neutrality. Politicians scurried to find a solution as hundreds of Kentuckians slipped out of state to join the contending armies.[6]

In August 1861, after Unionists won a majority in the state legislature, Federal officer William "Bull" Nelson established Camp Dick Robinson, a recruiting ground in Garrard County. Nelson also distributed muskets to pro-Union residents, and these actions convinced Southerners that the Bluegrass State was slipping from their grasp. Confederate General Leonidas Polk then took Columbus, Kentucky, a strategic point on the Mississippi River. In response, Union General Ulysses S. Grant seized Paducah. On September 7, the Unionist legislature ordered the Stars and Stripes hoisted over the state capitol. Four days later, they demanded that all Southern troops leave the commonwealth.[7]

Despite legislative directives, the Confederate commander in East Tennessee, Brigadier General Felix Kirk Zollicoffer, advanced into the Bluegrass State. Born in Maury County, Tennessee, on May 19, 1812, Zollicoffer was a former

Located in Garrard County, Kentucky, Camp Dick Robinson was an early Unionist recruiting ground. When Confederate General Felix Zollicoffer seized the Cumberland Gap, President Abraham Lincoln told a Northern governor, "I rather infer he did it because of his dread of Camp Dick Robinson." Some of the troops organized at the camp later fought at the Battle of Mill Springs. *Courtesy of the Kentucky Historical Society.*

newspaper editor and publisher. In 1835, he became state printer of Tennessee and married Louisa Gardner (who died in 1857, leaving Felix to raise their six children). A year later, Zollicoffer served as an officer in the Second Seminole War. Politically connected and horrifically nearsighted, Zollicoffer was Tennessee's adjutant general, the state comptroller, a Whig legislator and a six-term congressman. In 1860, he helped organize the Constitutional Union party, supported John Bell for president and was a representative to the Washington Peace Conference, which failed to prevent the Civil War.[8]

Confederate General Leonidas Polk seized Columbus, Kentucky, a move that Unionists believed violated Kentucky's neutrality. Polk's position at Columbus, a strategic point on the Mississippi River, represented the left flank of a Confederate defensive line that spanned across Kentucky. *Courtesy of the Library of Congress.*

Zollicoffer ultimately embraced secession, writing, "We must not, cannot, stand neutral and see our Southern brothers butchered." In May 1861, he was appointed brigadier general in the Provisional Army of Tennessee. Shortly thereafter, he was sent to East Tennessee, where he worked to consolidate Confederate control of the Unionist area.[9]

Zollicoffer recognized his lack of experience. That September, he wrote that "the responsibility is great. I feel my want of experience and knowledge of war for so large a command." Despite service in the Seminole War,

Confederate General Felix Zollicoffer was a prominent newspaper editor and politician in Tennessee before the Civil War. Zollicoffer commanded Rebel troops in East Tennessee and eastern Kentucky. He was killed at the Battle of Mill Springs. *Courtesy of the Library of Congress.*

Zollicoffer embodied the Civil War's numerous "political generals," who were, thanks to their antebellum political influence, appointed as officers. Historian Stanley Horn noted that the Tennessean "was totally lacking in military experience, and he had no formal training in that art...Zollicoffer was a valiant, magnetic, patriotic man, but as a commanding officer he was in a role for which he was unfitted." Despite his inexperience, Zollicoffer took the offensive.[10]

When Kentucky's neutrality ended, Unionists worked to gain control of the state. The Federal army moved its regional headquarters from Cincinnati to Louisville, and on September 10, Brigadier General George H. Thomas replaced "Bull" Nelson as commander of Camp Dick Robinson. Union soldier John Tuttle wrote, "The men had come to love General Nelson with all his brusque manners and were not well pleased with the change."[11]

Because of Thomas's Southern birth, Unionists eyed him with suspicion. Born in Southampton County, Virginia, on July 31, 1816, Thomas graduated from the U.S. Military Academy at West Point. Appointed second lieutenant in the 3rd U.S. Artillery, Thomas fought Seminoles in Florida and was recognized for gallantry during the Mexican War. Later, Thomas taught at West Point and fought Native Americans on the frontier. Although he was

Union General George H. Thomas led the Federal army at the Battle of Mill Springs. A Virginia native, Thomas's loyalty to the Union was confirmed after he led his troops to victory there. *Courtesy of the Library of Congress.*

a Virginian, he remained loyal to the Union and led a brigade in his home state in early 1861. That August, he was appointed brigadier general and was sent to the Bluegrass State. Upon his arrival at Camp Dick Robinson, he whipped the recruits into shape and prepared for a campaign into East Tennessee.[12]

Confederate General Albert Sidney Johnston commanded Department No. 2, a massive territory that spanned from the Appalachian Mountains beyond the Mississippi River. Johnston was later killed at the Battle of Shiloh, Tennessee. *Courtesy of the Library of Congress.*

The Confederates also worked to strengthen their influence in Kentucky. On September 10, Confederate General Albert Sidney Johnston was named commander of Department No. 2, a massive territory that spanned from the Appalachian Mountains beyond the Mississippi River. Four days later, Zollicoffer fortified the Cumberland Gap, the mountain pass that linked Tennessee, Kentucky and Virginia. He then moved troops to Cumberland Ford, located at present-day Pineville. Aware that Union troops were "threatening the invasion of East Tennessee," Zollicoffer told Kentucky governor Beriah Magoffin that he had seized the gap as a "precautionary movement" for "the safety of Tennessee." President Lincoln understood Zollicoffer's motives, telling a Northern governor, "I rather infer he did it because of his dread of Camp Dick Robinson."[13]

The Confederates soon advanced into Kentucky en masse. With Polk on the Mississippi River and Zollicoffer at Cumberland Ford, Johnston ordered General Simon B. Buckner to seize Bowling Green. The move established a Confederate defensive line across southern Kentucky. Polk held the left flank at Columbus, Buckner protected the center at Bowling Green and Zollicoffer held the right flank in eastern Kentucky with four thousand soldiers. Fort Henry on the Tennessee River and Fort Donelson on the Cumberland River in Tennessee provided extra support. Because the Confederates guarded a wide front, their four-hundred-mile line was tenuous at best. Moreover, Zollicoffer's position was weakened because many of the troops were poorly armed. In fact, antiquated weaponry helped doom the Confederate army at Mill Springs.[14]

Zollicoffer, who commanded 128 miles of the line, did not maintain a defensive posture. On September 19, he sent eight hundred Confederates to Barbourville, drove off the Union Home Guard and destroyed their camp. Shortly thereafter, Zollicoffer's troops bested Unionists in Laurel County and advanced into Clay County, where they sacked the Goose Creek Salt Works and took two hundred barrels of salt back to Cumberland Ford.[15]

After the Rebels struck Goose Creek, Thomas sent the 7th Kentucky Infantry and the 1st Kentucky Cavalry to the Rockcastle Hills near London, roughly thirty miles northwest of the salt works. There, they established Camp Wildcat. Located on a mountain near the road that connected the Cumberland Gap to central Kentucky, the troops at Camp Wildcat were to blunt any Confederate advance.[16]

In late 1862, artist Henry Moesler described the camp. "The scenery here is so beautiful and picturesque that my feeble thoughts and language cannot express," Moesler wrote. "Lofty & high Hills with beautifull [*sic*] Cliffs, nearly upright now and then sprinkled with a spot of Beautifull foliage." Nearly twelve months earlier, crackling volleys of musketry had shattered this idyllic scene.[17]

Zollicoffer decided to rout the enemy at Camp Wildcat before advancing into central Kentucky. With more than 3,500 troops, he fortified the passes around Cumberland Gap and then marched northward. On October 14, Brigadier General Albin Schoepf and the 14th Ohio, 17th Ohio and 33rd Indiana infantry regiments, and Battery B of the 1st Ohio Artillery reinforced Camp Wildcat. One member of the 1st Kentucky Cavalry called Schoepf "a Hungarian by birth, [and] a fine looking man, rather youthful looking for the position, and clean shaven, with the exception of a long waxed moustache parted in the middle, which gave him, notwithstanding his pleasant manners, a fierce warlike appearance." The Union troops needed more than looks, however, for the Confederates appeared at Camp Wildcat on October 21.[18]

Schoepf kept most of his command at the main campsite, but he posted four companies of the 33rd Indiana and the 1st Kentucky Cavalry on a ridge a half-mile away. Trooper Eastham Tarrant recalled that "a deep hollow" separated the two Union positions. When Zollicoffer reached the base of the mountain, he attacked the 33rd Indiana and 1st Kentucky

Confederate General Felix Zollicoffer seized and later fortified the Cumberland Gap, the mountain pass that links Kentucky, Virginia and Tennessee. This image shows the Cumberland Gap in 1862. *Courtesy of the Kentucky Historical Society.*

Cavalry with the 11th and 17th Tennessee infantry regiments. Tarrant peered down into "a narrow valley...[and] the whole bottom field...seemed to be swarming with live Rebels, on the march to attack our position." Repulsed, the Southerners then struck the main Union camp. Although the Confederates got to within fifty yards of the Federal line, they failed to take Camp Wildcat.[19]

Ample cover in the mountainous terrain kept casualties low. It is likely that the Confederates lost eleven killed and forty-two wounded while the

Federals suffered six killed and twenty-three wounded. Although Zollicoffer cancelled his invasion of central Kentucky, he hoped to renew the offensive. Tuttle remarked that Thomas assumed that Zollicoffer "had only fallen back to take a fresh start" and that the Rebel commander would "invade the state at some part farther west." Therefore, Thomas shifted his command to meet that threat. The Union officer moved his headquarters from Camp Dick Robinson to Crab Orchard, twenty-five miles to the south. He also deployed Schoepf to Somerset to watch Zollicoffer.[20]

This map from *Harper's Weekly* details important points related to the Mill Springs campaign, including Camp Dick Robinson, Somerset, London and Mill Springs. *Courtesy of the author.*

Having returned to Tennessee, Zollicoffer thought that the Federals would advance toward Albany or Monticello, Kentucky. Therefore, he shifted his command westward. He wrote to Johnston, "I propose to take and strengthen a position between Monticello and Somerset, Kentucky, giving us facilities for commanding the Cumberland River, the coal region supplying Nashville, &c."[21]

On November 12, Brigadier General William T. Sherman, the Union commander of Kentucky, panicked. Sherman feared that the Confederates were advancing northward toward Louisville or Lexington. He ordered

Union General Don Carlos Buell replaced General William T. Sherman as commander of Kentucky. Although the Lincoln administration pressured Buell to advance on East Tennessee, Buell instead hoped to capture Nashville. He did, however, order Union General George Thomas to move against Zollicoffer's Confederate army at Beech Grove. *Courtesy of the Library of Congress.*

Schoepf to fall back from Somerset to central Kentucky. Later called the "Wildcat Stampede," the withdrawal was a blow to Federal troops' morale. East Tennessee Union regiments, which hoped to rescue their home region, were especially furious. One soldier wrote that "some were lying prone on the ground sobbing, some stood on the highway swearing defiantly; others leaned against the fences sullenly, undetermined to move one way or the other." As the Federals plodded away from Somerset, one Union band played the "Dead March." Thomas, however, convinced Sherman that the Confederates were not advancing, and Schoepf was sent back to Somerset.[22]

Because of the Wildcat Stampede and because Sherman had claimed that hundreds of thousands of soldiers were needed to defend Kentucky, Union Brigadier General Don Carlos Buell replaced Sherman. Buell reorganized his army and put Thomas in command of his First Division. He then ordered Thomas to move from Crab Orchard toward Lebanon and Columbia so that Thomas's troops could be supplied from Louisville.[23]

Federal authorities pressured Buell to move on East Tennessee. General George McClellan, the Union general-in-chief, told Buell to send "something into East Tenna [*sic*] as promptly as possible." Buell, however, had other plans. With more than one-third of Kentucky under Confederate control, Buell made the capture of Nashville his primary objective. After taking the Tennessee capital, he would then move on East Tennessee. Nashville, Buell thought, was strategically more important. In addition, he could supply his troops by railroad rather than through the mountainous passes of eastern Kentucky. As Unionist R. M. Kelly explained, "Buell did not consider East Tennessee important enough to be his principal objective; he wanted it to be a subordinate feature in a great campaign." With Lincoln and McClellan pushing Buell to move on East Tennessee, Buell gave Thomas approval to advance against Zollicoffer.[24]

Just as the Union army had a command change, so, too, did the Confederates. On November 9, Major General George Bibb Crittenden was given command of Rebel forces in eastern Kentucky and East Tennessee. With this appointment, Crittenden commanded Zollicoffer's army.[25]

Born in Russellville, Kentucky, on March 20, 1812, George was the son of John J. Crittenden, who had been governor of Kentucky, U.S. attorney general and a U.S. senator. Before the Civil War, Senator Crittenden had offered a package of constitutional amendments—now known as the "Crittenden Compromise"—to end the sectional conflict. Those efforts failed, and Crittenden's family became divided by the war. George was raised in Frankfort, Kentucky, and educated in Lexington and the U.S. Military Academy at West Point. Upon his graduation in 1832, he became a lieutenant in the 4th U.S. Infantry, fought in the Black Hawk War and served in the Arkansas Territory and on the western frontier.[26]

As the son of a national politician, George could have had a promising career. A reputed addiction to alcohol, however, hindered his advancement. As early as the 1830s, Crittenden's father worried about his son's drinking. Historian Damon Eubank posits that Crittenden's greatest hurdle was his "lack of self-control." This flaw probably led to alcohol abuse while George served on the frontier, and alcoholism may have played a role in his leaving the

Confederate General George Bibb Crittenden was the son of U.S. Senator John J. Crittenden of Kentucky. Crittenden's family was divided during the Civil War. George was a Confederate general while another son, Thomas L. Crittenden, was a Union general. George commanded the Confederate army at the Battle of Mill Springs. *Courtesy of the Kentucky Historical Society.*

army in 1833. Once George resigned his commission, he returned to Kentucky before joining filibustering operations in Texas. In December 1842, Mexican soldiers took George prisoner, but he was released thanks to his father's influence. When the Mexican War officially started four years later, Crittenden was commissioned captain in the dragoons. Although he was arrested for drunkenness, he performed well in several battles. After the war, he was promoted to major, served in the West and secured a law degree. By early 1861, he was a lieutenant colonel in the U.S. army.[27]

When the Civil War began, George's father begged his son to remain with the Union. On April 30, 1861, the senator wrote to him, "Kentucky has not seceded, and I believe never will. She loves the Union, and will cling to it as long as possible. And so, I hope, will you. Be true to the government that has trusted in you, and stand fast to your nation's flag—the stars and stripes." Despite his father's wishes and his brother's service as a Union officer, George joined the Confederacy. Appointed brigadier general, he was likely assigned to eastern Kentucky and East Tennessee because he had more experience than Zollicoffer. In addition, Confederate authorities hoped that Crittenden's name—which carried great weight in the Bluegrass State—would rally men to the Southern standard. Although some Rebel officers were unimpressed with the choice, by late November 1861, Crittenden was on his way to Knoxville to assume command.[28]

Chapter 2

Zollicoffer again entered Kentucky in late November 1861. Marching toward Albany, he issued a proclamation explaining why he had returned. "We march into Kentucky for the purpose of defending the people of a sister Southern State, against an invading Northern army and their federal adherents," Zollicoffer wrote. Understanding that some Kentuckians supported the Confederacy, the commander told his troops to respect private property. "A few bad men must not be permitted to bring reproach upon the whole command," the general explained, "or by lawless acts to convert the people of Kentucky from friends into enemies."[29]

With Schoepf's return to Somerset, Zollicoffer moved to block a potential Federal advance. On November 27, he sent troops to Mill Springs, Kentucky, located on the south side of the Cumberland River, approximately fifteen miles southwest of Somerset. Zollicoffer reported that Mill Springs, with high riverbank bluffs protecting the site, offered a good defensive position. He also noted the prevalence of timber and water and reported that the location was "capable of easy defense, commanding the ferry. Geographically, it is the best position on this side of the river for commanding the approaches to Cumberland Gap and Jacksborough," Tennessee. Mill Springs could be resupplied by boat from Nashville, forage was plentiful and mills were nearby. Therefore, he reported, "it is probable a good position may be found there for winter quarters." Union troops, who feared a northward advance, sank boats to deter the Rebels from crossing the river. "From this camp as a base of operations," Zollicoffer

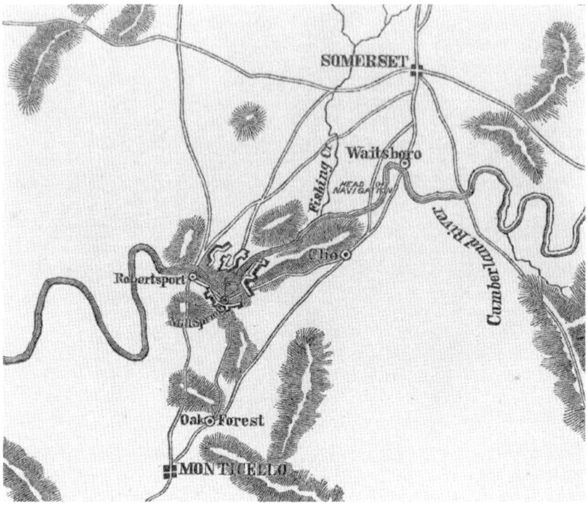

Left: "Map of Mill Spring and the Vicinity." *Courtesy of the Kentucky Historical Society.*

Below: The high bluffs that surround the Cumberland River are evident in this post-war photograph. *Courtesy of the Kentucky Historical Society.*

explained, "I hope in mild weather to penetrate the country toward London or Danville." By late November, Zollicoffer had approximately 3,500 men at Mill Springs. Many of them, however, were unarmed while others had only flintlocks and shotguns.[30]

Just as Confederate troops defended a broad front, so, too, did the Federals, who were dispersed. On November 29, Thomas arrived in Lebanon, where he had four infantry regiments, an artillery battery and two other regiments nearby. Union Colonel Samuel Carter was in London with three regiments, two units were posted in Columbia, one Hoosier regiment was in Crab Orchard, Camp Dick Robinson held one regiment and an artillery battery and closest to Zollicoffer, near Somerset, were two regiments and an artillery battery. Concerned about Zollicoffer's presence at Mill Springs, Thomas sent two regiments and several cannons to Somerset. Buell, however, who still hoped for a spring campaign against Nashville, recalled one of the regiments. "From Buell's perspective," historian Larry Daniel notes, "Zollicoffer was more nuisance than threat." Therefore, Schoepf was urged to entrench at Somerset while a cavalry regiment was sent there to perform reconnaissance duties.[31]

Schoepf was thankful for the reinforcements. On December 1, his troops skirmished with Rebels near Fishing Creek, west of Somerset. The next day, the Confederates returned with four cannons and drove off the Northerners. Schoepf reported that the Cumberland River was no barrier. Although water levels were high, the Rebels could "cross anywhere" on flatboats that they had constructed.[32]

These skirmishes and praise from his superiors emboldened Zollicoffer. On December 4, he was told that his movements were met "with great satisfaction. Every move is entirely approved." The next day, without permission, he crossed troops over the Cumberland River to Beech Grove, just north of Mill Springs. There, he established his winter camp.[33]

Zollicoffer believed that Beech Grove was a defensible position. Moreover, crossing the Cumberland placed his troops closer to the enemy at Somerset and allowed him to respond to their movements. One writer called the area "an eminence protected on its rear and flanks by the river, and with about 1,200 yards of fighting front to defend." In fact, the camp was protected on three sides. The Cumberland River formed a "horseshoe" shape on the south and east side of Beech Grove while White Oak Creek covered Zollicoffer's eastern, or left, flank. The river and creek flowed in deep ravines, making a crossing extremely difficult. Upon reaching Beech Grove, the Rebels cleared a field of fire, dug entrenchments and built 150 cabins. Zollicoffer, a man

This *Harper's Weekly* image from March 1862 details the cabins that Zollicoffer's Rebels constructed at Beech Grove. After the Battle of Mill Springs, Union troops occupied, and later destroyed, this site. *Courtesy of the Kentucky Historical Society.*

with no military schooling and little experience, did not consider the dangers of placing his soldiers' backs to the Cumberland River.[34]

Zollicoffer soon had seven infantry regiments, eight cannons and eighteen cavalry companies at Beech Grove, numbering 5,500 men. His immediate priority was the construction of the earthworks and cabins. A member of the 19th Tennessee remarked that this left little time for regimental drill, and "as for brigade drill, such a thing had not been done. Here we were too busy building breastworks and quarters to think of drilling." Zollicoffer continued to probe Union lines. The men appreciated these movements, prompting the *Richmond Daily Dispatch* to comment that "the army under Gen. Zollicoffer are reported to have entire confidence in him, and are eager to be led against the invaders."[35]

Movements toward Somerset led to skirmishes. On December 7, the 35th Ohio fought Confederate cavalry three miles west of town, resulting in six casualties. Although Schoepf had received additional horsemen, he was unhappy with them. He blamed the Rebels' ability to approach his lines on his lack of trained troopers and reported that "the cavalry under my command, as usual, behaved badly. They are a nuisance, and the sooner they are disbanded the better." He added that they were "lounging about the villages and drinking establishments," bothering citizens. The next day brought additional skirmishes near Fishing Creek. The Rebels pushed the Northerners toward Somerset, more than a dozen men were killed and wounded and seventeen Federals were captured. Schoepf, who had ten cannons and five thousand men in Somerset, requested additional reinforcements. Thomas urged sending a brigade there from London, but Buell refused. "The affairs at Somerset are annoying," Buell wrote, "but I do not intend to be diverted more than necessary from more important purposes. I [suppose that] Schoepf will be able to drive the enemy across the river again." Other Union officers were not so confident. Brigadier General Jeremiah Boyle predicted that if Zollicoffer was not forced across the Cumberland, "the enemy will be in the center of the state." On December 9, Carter reinforced Schoepf with two regiments of East Tennessee Unionists.[36]

Zollicoffer soon reported that he was "rapidly strengthening the defenses" at Beech Grove. His superiors, however, were dismayed that he had crossed the river. In fact, Crittenden was ignorant of the movement. Although Crittenden had arrived in Knoxville in early December, President Jefferson Davis had called him to Richmond, Virginia, to discuss East Tennessee. Therefore, an absent Crittenden was unable to pull Zollicoffer back across the river.[37]

Upon learning that his superiors disapproved of the move, Zollicoffer explained his reasons. "I infer from [your dispatch] that I should not have crossed the river, but it is now too late," he wrote. "My means of recrossing is so limited I should hardly accomplish it in [the] face of the enemy." Zollicoffer asserted that "this camp is immediately opposite to Mill Springs...The river protects our rear and flanks. We have about 1,200 yards [of] fighting front to defend, which we are intrenching [*sic*]." He added that "the position I occupy north of the river is a fine basis for operations in front. It is a much stronger natural position for defense than that on the south side." He also explained, "I will endeavor to prevent the forces at Columbia [Thomas] and Somerset [Schoepf] from uniting." Zollicoffer hoped to respond to enemy movements and keep the Union forces in the region divided.[38]

On December 10, Brigadier General William Carroll's brigade was ordered to Zollicoffer's army. Many of Carroll's men were unarmed, and those troops remained in Knoxville until they could procure weapons. Carroll's predicament is illustrative of Confederate arms deficiencies in East Tennessee. Five days earlier, Carroll had asked for rifles that were stored at Columbus, noting, "I have here 1,700 men, only 400 armed." The weapons, however, were earmarked for Johnston at Bowling Green. Carroll's need was great. The 38th Tennessee, which numbered 998 men, had only 250 guns, including muskets, rifles and shotguns, but only 50 of these were in good condition. In addition, the 39th Tennessee had 771 men armed with 200 muskets, shotguns and rifles that were "mostly unfit for use except in an emergency." Another unit was only "partially armed with old country rifles and shot-guns." The 16th Alabama was also armed with flintlock muskets. Crittenden later noted that Carroll had one regiment in which the weapons were "wholly unserviceable and most of the remainder unfit for service." He added that "the men had some old flint-lock muskets, some squirrel rifles with saber-bayonets and some without, and some shot-guns, almost all out of fix and wholly unfit for service." These arms deficiencies would haunt Carroll's command at the Battle of Mill Springs.[39]

When Crittenden learned that Zollicoffer had crossed the Cumberland, he immediately ordered the Tennessean to return to the south side of the river. With Zollicoffer outnumbered if the Federals consolidated, Crittenden worried about the troops having their backs to the water. Zollicoffer, however, told Crittenden that he could not return because the river was flooded. Although Crittenden was "dissatisfied," he "knew that the General had been actuated by pure motives, [so] I accepted his excuse."[40]

Crittenden believed that the Cumberland River, "with high, muddy banks, was a troublesome barrier in the rear of Beech Grove." Historian Brian McKnight contends that Crittenden's concerns came from his experiences as a filibusterer in Mexico. In 1842, McKnight wrote, Crittenden crossed the Rio Grande and was hit by Mexican troops at Mier, Mexico. As the Americans were "trapped with the river at their back, [and] the Mexican army in their front…They quickly surrendered." Crittenden worried because the earthworks at Beech Grove were "incomplete and insufficient." The site was also surrounded by "commanding positions" that would allow enemy artillery to fire into the works.[41]

Although Zollicoffer hoped for a spring offensive, he complained that he needed supplies and reinforcements. He had five regiments at Beech Grove and two regiments at Mill Springs, and he called for additional troops. Three days later, Captain Hugh L.W. McClung's Tennessee artillery, which included six guns, and Colonel William Wood's 16th Alabama Infantry arrived south of the Cumberland. Colonel Samuel Powell's 29th Tennessee also marched toward the river. By New Year's Eve, Zollicoffer had seven infantry regiments, three battalions and four companies of cavalry, as well as two seven-gun artillery batteries, numbering 6,154 men.[42]

Zollicoffer also faced difficulties in procuring supplies from Nashville. While foraging expeditions secured some food, including turkeys, chickens, eggs and butter, his troops were low on blankets and other necessities. Confederate Colonel David Cummings wrote to his wife, "We are working on our winter quarters and expect to be able to command the River from here down. When Lincums [*sic*] minions get too close to the river we expect to send out expeditions to drive them back." He asked his wife to send him a bottle of black cordial, "cologne," pickles, ink, matches and four dozen coat buttons. He added, "I do not look for much more hard fighting." He was certainly mistaken. Within weeks, the Rebels would face fierce fighting indeed.[43]

Chapter 3

With Zollicoffer's earthworks on the north side of the Cumberland River, Schoepf tested the Rebel lines with a reconnaissance in force. On December 18, he left Somerset with five infantry regiments and six cannons. The artillery, however, had difficulty traveling over the rough roads and was left behind. Three miles from Beech Grove, they skirmished with Confederate cavalry. The Southerners, Schoepf reported, would not leave their works "for a field fight." He added that the Rebel position "can only be taken at the point of the bayonet under many disadvantages, and a probable heavy loss of life on our side." Concerned that the roads hindered his ability to use artillery against the earthworks, Schoepf lobbied against making a frontal assault. Instead, he proposed crossing the Cumberland, positioning artillery upon bluffs on the south side of the river and then bombarding Beech Grove. Schoepf returned to Somerset convinced that Zollicoffer would remain in his works and that "nothing would be gained by taking his fortified position." One of Schoepf's aides, Kentuckian Green Clay, also thought that Zollicoffer "will not attack, tho we are always ready for him."[44]

While Schoepf scouted the Rebel position, Thomas, sixty-five miles to the northwest in Lebanon, organized his command. James Moore of the 10th Indiana, noting that his unit had been brigaded with Kentucky and Ohio regiments, claimed that his comrades composed the "best drilled regiment there is about this place except the 9th Ohio they are a little better than we are." Hoosier Wesley Elmore was unhappy to serve with Kentuckians. "There is great dissatisfaction...among the troops on account of this," Elmore wrote. He added, "We do not wish to Be Rushed into Battle with a Parcel of Green Kentuckians...There is one Kentucky Regiment Here who do not know A Right Face from a left[.]" Elmore, who incorrectly believed that the Virginia-born Thomas was from Indiana, noted, "And more than this we wish to Fight if Fight we must under a Hoosier General but we will probably have to submit to our fate."[45]

Although Buell discounted Zollicoffer's presence near Somerset, he did not want Rebels on his left flank when he advanced on Bowling Green. Therefore, on December 29, Buell ordered Thomas to link with Schoepf to drive Zollicoffer out of Kentucky. Buell did not want the movement to turn into an invasion of East Tennessee, so he told Thomas to stay north of the Cumberland River. Thomas and Schoepf were to meet west of Somerset, and Buell directed, "The movement should be made rapidly and secretly, and the blow should be vigorous and decided." Buell wanted a two-pronged advance, with Thomas hitting Zollicoffer's left flank while Schoepf struck the Confederates' front. Thomas's advance units left Lebanon on December 31. The army consisted of Colonel Mahlon Manson's 2nd Brigade, which included the 4th Kentucky, 10th Kentucky, 10th Indiana and 14th Ohio infantry regiments and two regiments from Colonel Robert McCook's brigade, the 2nd Minnesota and 9th Ohio. Joining these troops were Colonel Frank Wolford's 1st Kentucky Cavalry and Battery C of the 1st Ohio Light Artillery, led by Captain Dennis Kenny.[46]

Minnesotan Judson Bishop remarked that although the army left Lebanon "with bands playing and colors displayed," bad weather and terrible roads made it a miserable trek. Despite the difficulties, another member of the regiment wrote, "we had great confidence in ourselves and our generals and looked forward to the end of our march without a doubt of complete success." Although the army—laden with six hundred wagons—made good progress from Lebanon to Columbia, it started to rain and then sleet, and the dirt roads turned into mud. One Indiana soldier recalled that "all will agree that the worst roads on the face of the earth at that time were between Columbia and [Somerset]. The mules sank to their bellies, and wagons to their axles, details were made to help the teams along, but our progress was very slow." Hoosier Derrick Harrison concurred, describing them as "the worse [*sic*] roads I ever saw."[47]

While the Union soldiers endured the difficult march, Confederate commanders worried about the placement of Zollicoffer's army.

Schoepf's reconnaissance in force had shown that the Federals were willing to press toward the Rebel works. Therefore, Crittenden wanted his men back across the river. On January 3, Crittenden arrived at Mill Springs and assumed command. Shocked to still find Zollicoffer north of the river, he immediately ordered rafts to be built, but poor weather hampered construction.[48]

The weather also disheartened the Rebel troops. "This is a terrible morning," Colonel Cummings wrote. "We have had rain two or three days and a little snow last night. It appears to be turning cold with some wind. It is hard work to live in any comfort in camp." Although the steamer *Noble Ellis* arrived from Nashville on January 7 with food, sugar, molasses and other supplies, discontent reigned. Colonel W.S. Statham of the 15th Mississippi, for example, wanted his regiment transferred to Bowling Green. Confederate authorities demurred, however, telling him that "the position of General Zollicoffer is too important and too exposed to permit of any reduction of force." At the time, Zollicoffer's army consisted of eight infantry regiments, four infantry battalions, two cavalry companies and two artillery companies. Shortly thereafter, Brigadier General William Carroll's troops reached the area. They were still poorly armed, and their arrival immediately before the Battle of Mill Springs signified that the Confederate army was never fully integrated when the shooting started.[49]

In Somerset, Schoepf knew that reinforcements had reached Beech Grove. Still hoping to bombard the works from south of the river, the Hungarian reported that an attacking force would have to advance across a narrow strip of land toward strong entrenchments. In addition, the Confederates had cut trees north of their works to create a tangled abatis for three-quarters of a mile. Schoepf noted that "there is no approach except by the narrow road in front, while the hope of a flank movement is futile, as the precipitous bluffs of the Cumberland upon the east and those of White Oak Creek upon the west render a flank movement of infantry impossible." The Beech Grove position was impregnable to a direct assault, Schoepf argued, and doing so "must be attended with heavy loss of life on our part." Schoepf's concerns, however, were ignored. Thomas reminded him that Buell—who was ignorant of the terrain and believed Schoepf's plan to be too complicated—had already given the order. Schoepf's aide, however, was optimistic. Green Clay wrote to his father, "So the plan that is now to be pursued is for an advance on this side of the river, & I have no doubt it will but result in driving him across...If Zollicoffer escapes by recrossing the river, it will not be the fault of Gen. Schoepf."[50]

This twentieth-century postcard of the Cumberland River highlights the tall bluffs along the banks of the river. *Courtesy of the Kentucky Historical Society.*

Despite Schoepf's worries, he did not keep his men confined to Somerset. On January 8, his troops bagged two Southern cavalrymen near Fishing Creek. The skirmishing continued, prompting Union trooper J. A. Brents to write, "We were continually scouting and skirmishing with the enemy in the direction of Mill Springs." In order to prevent the Beech Grove camp from being supplied, Union Brigadier General Jeremiah Boyle blocked the Cumberland River "at Horse Shoe bottom near Jamestown" with artillery and infantry units. Boyle happily informed one Kentucky politician that "no more steamers will pass up."[51]

Thomas's men, slowly slogging through the muddy roads, finally neared Somerset. On January 15, Colonel Robert McCook informed Thomas that the 1st Kentucky Cavalry was scouting near Logan's Crossroads, a farm owned by William Logan located ten miles north of Beech Grove and eight miles west of Somerset. Although the horsemen found no Rebels, McCook added, "If he comes this way we can whip all of them without any trouble in the position we have."[52]

Two days later, Thomas reached Logan's Crossroads with the 9th Ohio, 2nd Minnesota, 10th Indiana and Kenny's artillery battery. The Union commander stopped at Logan's farm to await Captain Henry S. Wetmore's battery and the 4th Kentucky, 10th Kentucky, 14th Ohio and 18th

U.S. Regulars, who were delayed by the bad roads. Logan's farm consisted of a few cabins, some fields and hilly, wooded ground. One veteran noted that the area "was undulating and mostly covered with thick woods and brush, with some small open fields inclosed [*sic*] by the usual rail fence of the country." The farm was located at the crossroads of the Columbia-Somerset road, which ran east to west, and the Mill Springs road, which ran from north to south. Because some of Thomas's regiments were delayed, he asked Schoepf to send him the 12th Kentucky, 1st Tennessee and 2nd Tennessee infantry regiments and William Standart's Battery B of the 1st Ohio Light Artillery from Somerset, all of which had to cross Fishing Creek to reach the crossroads.[53]

Upon his arrival, Thomas learned that a Confederate forage train was approximately six miles away. Therefore, he ordered the 14th Ohio and 10th Kentucky to capture the Rebel wagons. Thomas then established his headquarters on the Somerset–Columbia road, about three-fourths of a mile west of Logan's farm. His regiments, spread out around different water sources, bivouacked apart from one another. The 4th Kentucky and part of the 1st Ohio Artillery camped near the intersection, facing south toward Beech Grove. The 10th Indiana and three companies of the 1st Kentucky Cavalry were placed nearly a mile farther south. They were deployed, cavalryman Eastham Tarrant wrote, on "the main road leading to the enemy's camp." The 9th Ohio and 2nd Minnesota were three-fourths of a mile off to the right. To watch for any Rebel advance, Thomas sent "strong pickets" southward, including two companies of the 10th Indiana and cavalry pickets from the 1st Kentucky Cavalry.[54]

When Crittenden learned that Union forces were converging approximately ten miles away, the Confederate commander consolidated his divided force. The 17th Tennessee, 28th Tennessee, 37th Tennessee, several cavalry companies and four artillery pieces were at Mill Springs. At Beech Grove, north of the river, were the 15th Mississippi, 16th Alabama, 19th Tennessee, 20th Tennessee, 25th Tennessee, 29th Tennessee, additional cavalry battalions and twelve artillery pieces. Crittenden rightfully assumed that Thomas and Schoepf would link before they advanced on his position, and he estimated that this combined enemy force would number between six and ten thousand troops. The officer also knew that recent rains had raised Fishing Creek. With the water rising, he hoped that Schoepf's troops in Somerset would have difficulty reaching Thomas.[55]

At daylight on January 18, Crittenden ordered his soldiers at Mill Springs to Beech Grove. "I am threatened by a superior force of the enemy in front," he informed Johnston, "and finding it impossible to cross the river I will have to make the fight on the ground I now occupy." Just as the rains had raised Fishing Creek, the Cumberland River was also high. Crittenden believed that his fears of fighting a battle with his back to a swollen river were about to be realized. "Here was thrust upon me the very contingency which my order to General Zollicoffer [to recross the river] was intended to obviate," he later wrote.[56]

Corporal Nicholas M. Wayman, 1st Kentucky (Union) Cavalry. Approximately 250 members of Wayman's regiment fought at Mill Springs. *Courtesy of the Kentucky Historical Society.*

Just as Crittenden feared, Union forces met at Logan's Crossroads. On January 18, the 4th Kentucky Infantry, a battalion of the Michigan Engineers and Mechanics, and Wetmore's artillery battery of two howitzers and two Parrott Rifles arrived and camped near the 10th Indiana. Although Fishing Creek was flooded, Schoepf's three infantry regiments and an artillery battery crossed and joined Thomas's army. Upon their arrival, Thomas's command increased to more than five thousand men. For Schoepf's troops, it was a rough night. Their wagons could not cross Fishing Creek, so they camped in the rain without tents. Minnesotan Judson Bishop called it the "darkest night and the coldest and most pitiless and persistent rain we ever knew." Bishop, however, took comfort in the fact that the Rebels were "at least as wet and cold and wretched as he was himself." As rain pelted the soldiers, one member of the 10th Indiana noted, "We slept on our arms prepared for work at short notice." The Rebels were close, so the Federals took no chances.[57]

Perhaps the most worried of Thomas's troops were companies E and G of the 10th Indiana, who were deployed as pickets south of the crossroads. Moreover, "a strong advanced picket of Cavalry," which included Company C of the 1st Kentucky, was farther south at a creek called Timmy's Branch. Once during the night, the jittery pickets fired shots along the picket line.

The false alarm stirred the Union camp, and the 10th Indiana formed a battle line. The Hoosiers stood in the rain until their officers, realizing there was no danger, sent them back to their tents. Shortly thereafter, those nervous pickets were replaced by companies I and K. Company I deployed a mile from the Union camp, Company K was posted an additional three hundred yards farther south and the Kentucky cavalrymen were down the Mill Springs road at Timmy's Branch. The troops remained nervous. They had good reason.[58]

Chapter 4

On January 18, a secessionist citizen told Crittenden what the Confederate commander already suspected: the Federals were divided, but they would soon link and attack. The civilian told Crittenden where Thomas was camped, but wrongly reported that Schoepf's soldiers were blocked by a flooded Fishing Creek. Thinking that Thomas and Schoepf were divided, Crittenden decided to take the offensive and crush the Union forces in detail. He would break Thomas before Schoepf could join him.[59]

Crittenden's aggressiveness was also driven by his army's lack of supplies. "Absolute want of the necessary provisions to feed my command was pressing," he wrote. "The country around was barren or exhausted." With Boyle blocking the Cumberland River, supplies from Nashville were cut off. In addition, his back was to the river, and Crittenden believed that the Beech Grove defenses were incomplete and thereby indefensible. He did not, however, return to Mill Springs to defend that position. With the army's horses and equipment at Beech Grove, a lack of boats prevented Crittenden from crossing the animals and baggage. Moreover, Crittenden feared that Thomas would fall upon them while they were in transit and at their most vulnerable. Therefore, he would fight on the north side of the river.[60]

As a West Point graduate with antebellum military experience, Crittenden would have been familiar with two important military maxims. First, never fight with your back to a river, and second, strike your enemy while he is divided and then defeat him piecemeal. As noted, Crittenden had previously been captured in Mexico after being trapped with his back to the water.

Refusing to repeat this mistake, he was determined to fight a divided enemy away from Beech Grove, which he believed to be an untenable position with incomplete defenses chosen by the amateur Zollicoffer. Crittenden would strike Thomas before Schoepf arrived. This strategy was repeated multiple times during the Civil War, with one example occurring just three months after Mill Springs. In April 1862, in what proved to be the Battle of Shiloh, Johnston attacked Grant at Pittsburg Landing, Tennessee, before more troops led by "Bull" Nelson arrived. Crittenden knew that if he crossed the river, Thomas and Schoepf would link anyway, leaving him with a more formidable opponent. If he stayed in the works, he feared that the Federals would simply cross the river and bombard Beech Grove from the south bank. With little food and forage, he could not withstand a siege. Therefore, military maxims pointed to the most logical choice. He would move from his works and attack a divided enemy.

Crittenden later reported that "the enemy sought evidently to combine their forces stationed at Somerset [Schoepf] and Columbia [Thomas], and, when such a junction was made, to invest my intrenchments [*sic*]. I deemed it proper, therefore, to make an attack before the junction could be effected, feeling confident, from the reports of the cavalry pickets, made at a late hour, that the waters of Fishing Creek were so high as to prevent them from uniting." This was, however, inadequate intelligence. Crittenden did not know that Schoepf's three regiments and an artillery battery, all led by brigade commander Colonel Samuel P. Carter, had already joined Thomas at Logan's Crossroads.[61]

On the night of January 18, Crittenden held a council of war with his brigade and regimental commanders. Crittenden presented three options. First, they could try to retreat to the south side of the river, but they had few boats. Second, they could defend Beech Grove, but Crittenden believed the works were too incomplete to withstand a Federal assault. Third, they could strike Thomas before he was reinforced. Afraid that Thomas would strike while they were crossing the Cumberland, and unwilling to fight with his back to the river when the Union troops could cross elsewhere, Crittenden endorsed the third option. All officers reputedly agreed with their commander's assessment. Crittenden later wrote that "there was not one of them who did not concur with me in the opinion that Thomas must be attacked immediately, and, if possible, by surprise." Rumors later spread that Zollicoffer and Colonel David Cummings of the 19th Tennessee opposed the idea of attacking. These reports, however, likely sprung up as a postwar defense of Zollicoffer, as the Confederates made excuses for their ultimate defeat. In a letter written by

Cummings shortly after the battle, he noted that all of them "unanimously agreed" to attack. Another post-battle rumor—that Crittenden and Carroll were drunk during the council—gained more credence and damaged the commander's already fragile reputation.[62]

Crittenden's five thousand soldiers left Beech Grove at midnight on January 18. Most of them were inexperienced, poorly drilled and inadequately equipped. Since many of Crittenden's men were clad in blue uniforms, he told them to use the password "Kentucky" if they were unsure of whom they were facing. Crittenden hoped that this password would allow them to recognize one another and would prevent friendly-fire casualties.[63]

As the men marched out of the works, Zollicoffer reputedly shouted that "he would take them to Indiana, or go to hell himself!" Although this promise may have briefly boosted their morale, the Rebels' ardor faded as rain turned the roads into a churning mess. Carroll noted that "the night was dark and gloomy; a cold rain was constantly descending, rendering the march extremely difficult and unpleasant." With the mud sometimes twelve inches deep, it took the Confederates six hours to march less than ten miles. James L. Cooper of the 20th Tennessee lamented, "We had had much rain, and the roads were in a terrible condition." A member of the 19th Tennessee concurred, writing that "the night was dark and cold, and the bitter winds drove the sleet and rain in our faces, yet on we went, plodding in the gloom and mud."[64]

Zollicoffer's brigade led the march, leaving thirty minutes before Carroll's brigade. A mile initially separated the two units, but that distance grew as the roads deteriorated and artillery pieces became stuck in the mud. Zollicoffer's brigade was led by his cavalry, consisting of Captain T. C. Saunders's and Captain William Bledsoe's independent cavalry companies. Next followed Zollicoffer's infantry. The 15th Mississippi, commanded by Lieutenant Colonel Edward Walthall, the only Rebel regiment armed with rifled muskets, led the way. Behind the Mississippians were Cummings's 19th Tennessee, Colonel Joel Battle's 20th Tennessee and Colonel Sidney Stanton's 25th Tennessee. Zollicoffer's artillery, consisting of four guns of Captain A. M. Rutledge's battery, followed the infantry. Carroll's brigade trudged behind Zollicoffer's men and consisted of Lieutenant Colonel Thomas C. H. Miller's 17th Tennessee, Colonel John Murray's 28th Tennessee and Colonel Samuel Powell's 29th Tennessee. These troops were followed by Captain Hugh L. W. McClung's battery of two guns. Colonel William Wood's 16th Alabama marched in the rear as a reserve, followed by two cavalry battalions led by lieutenant colonels B. M. Branner and George R. McClellan.[65]

Because of the rain, the mud and the troops' inexperience, the Confederate attack plan was simple. They would advance northward up the Mill Springs road, toward Logan's Crossroads. When they met the Federals, the lead regiments would deploy on either side of the road and attack, using the lane as a guide.

At daylight on January 19, after marching all night, Zollicoffer's horsemen encountered the pickets of the 1st Kentucky Cavalry along Timmy's Branch, the small creek that crossed the Mill Springs Road about three miles south of Logan's Crossroads. Despite the previous night's false alarm spread by the 10th Indiana's pickets, the Kentuckians were alert. One of these scouts, a trooper named "Big Horse" Logan, had local connections. Tarrant wrote that Logan was "a worthy descendant of the Indian fighting Logans who lived in the days of Boone. He was fighting on his own family's soil, as the battle took place in Logan's fields." The Rebel cavalry hit the Kentucky horsemen, and musketry sputtered across Timmy's Branch. At least two Federals were injured, including Russell Smith and Isaac Cole, who died later that night. The Kentuckians fell back toward the two companies of the 10th Indiana, which were posted nearly a mile up the road. Upon hearing the gunfire, the Hoosiers shouted a warning to their comrades. Thanks to the 1st Kentucky's alert pickets, Crittenden noted, "the attack as a surprise failed; nevertheless it was promptly made."[66]

The dismounted Kentucky cavalry rushed northward toward their mounts. Their colonel, Frank Wolford, reported, "When we reached our horses we found them surrounded by the enemy. I cut them loose and let them run down the road, when my men caught them and remounted, the enemy getting two or three of our horses." The cavalry slowly fell back toward the Hoosier pickets, sometimes dismounting to contend with the Rebel advance, once halting near a log house on the west side of the lane.[67]

The Confederates pressed up the Mill Springs Road. When they neared the Union pickets, they piled up blankets, knapsacks and other equipment before the lead regiments deployed into battle lines. The 1st Kentucky Cavalry and Company K of the 10th Indiana, posted about three hundred yards south of Company I, fell back, firing to slow the Southern advance. In one instance, Hoosier George Shortle of Company K was accidently left behind. Alone, Shortle ran when the Confederates appeared. Thirty Rebels shot at him but missed. According to Derrick Harrison of the 10th Indiana, Shortle "then stopped and pulled off his boots and made his escape. This was close work and a joke on the boots dont [*sic*] you think?" The two

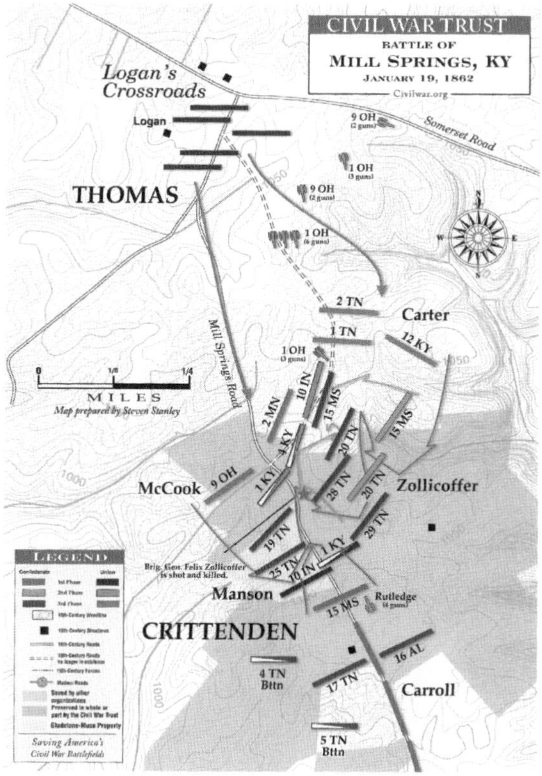

Left: The Civil War Trust's map of the Battle of Mill Springs. *Courtesy of the Civil War Trust.*

Below: This drawing from a wartime patriotic cover (envelope) shows the skirmishers of the 15th Mississippi approaching the pickets of the 10th Indiana Infantry. *Courtesy of the Kentucky Historical Society.*

Indiana companies fell back, linked near a cabin behind a hill on the west side of the road and prepared for the Rebels to crest the ridge. To counter the pickets, Zollicoffer deployed companies E and G of the 15th Mississippi and put them into a loose skirmish line. Lieutenant James Binford of the 15th Mississippi remarked that "both companies had been thoroughly drilled as Zouave skirmishers, being deployed about eight paces apart, advanced in beautiful order and were soon under fire from the skirmishers sent out by the 10th Indiana." As gunfire rolled through the foggy morning, the Confederate advance stalled as Zollicoffer halted that regiment and called up the two companies of skirmishers.[68]

The Confederates were wise to lead their army with the 15th Mississippi. Organized in Corinth, the regiment had colorful company names that reflected either their hometowns or respected officers. Company A was the Long Creek Rifles; Company B from Carroll County was the Winona Stars; Company C was the Quitman Rifles; Company D from Choctaw County was the Wigfall Rifles; Carroll County's Company E was the McClung Rifles; companies F, G and H were from Yalobusha County and were the Water Valley Rifle Guards, the Grenada Rifles and the Yalobusha Rifles, respectively; Company I from Choctaw County was the Choctaw Guards; Company K was the Oktibbeha Plough Boys from Oktibbeha County and the Choctaw Grays. These troops, who had fought at Camp Wildcat, were likely in the advance because they were the only unit armed with rifled muskets and were therefore the best-equipped regiment. The other Confederate units were armed with flintlock muskets that fired "buck and ball" rounds consisting of one musket ball and three smaller buckshot.[69]

Major Delmore Miller of the 10th Indiana had posted the pickets approximately a mile south of his regiment's camp. Company K was a quarter mile beyond Company I. If attacked, Company K was to fall back on the other company. Then, if pressed, they were to withdraw to their camp. When the Rebels appeared, the Hoosiers followed this plan and joined forces at the cabin on the west side of the road. Although Zollicoffer's brigade was at their front, the two Hoosier companies—numbering about two hundred men—stood their ground because they were not overwhelmed by the enemy. Poor roads had separated Zollicoffer's regiments, leaving the 15th Mississippi far in the lead. Therefore, the two Indiana companies initially faced only one of Zollicoffer's regiments. Zollicoffer was also unsure of how many Federals he faced. So, instead of rolling over the pickets, he deployed the two companies of the 15th Mississippi as skirmishers to probe the Union line. With the troops obscured in the fog, they simply fired at muzzle flashes in the distance. One member of the 19th Tennessee wrote that the black powder smoke was "beaten back by the rain and, setting on the ground, increased the gloom." Once the Mississippians pressed ahead, however, the pickets fell back and likely stopped on a narrow ridge about two hundred yards north of the cabin. Ravines immediately south of their line helped protect their flanks. The retreat through the fog, however, was a dangerous proposition. Two members of the 10th Indiana were "run over by a cavalryman" and injured when the 1st Kentucky fell back. After causing the injuries, Wolford's horsemen dismounted on the hill, which was, Wolford wrote, "commanding a field through which the enemy were advancing."[70]

Although Zollicoffer faced only pickets, he did not send the entire 15th Mississippi forward to crush the two Hoosier companies. Peering through the fog at muzzle flashes, the nearsighted brigade commander was unsure of what he faced. Therefore, he halted the 15th Mississippi and awaited his other regiments. When more troops reached the hill south of the cabin, Zollicoffer ordered his men into battle lines. This maneuver took more time as his inexperienced men deployed in the fog over unfamiliar ground. Zollicoffer formed two lines, with the 19th Tennessee on the left, or the west side, of the lane and the 15th Mississippi on the right side of the road. The 25th Tennessee moved behind the 19th Tennessee and the 20th Tennessee formed behind the 15th Mississippi. Upon taking position, Cooper, of the 20th Tennessee, noted, "The fight had commenced in earnest, and we were under fire directly."[71]

From the Rebel left flank, one member of the 19th Tennessee endured the Hoosiers' fire. "The balls began passing over our heads pretty fast with a zip, zip," a soldier wrote, "but they did not seem to be doing any harm for they were two hundred yards away on the hill above us." There were some casualties, however, with Captain C. G. Armistead of the 15th Mississippi falling among the wounded.[72]

The soldiers in the Union camps a mile to the north heard the gunfire. A captain in the 2nd Minnesota heard "a musket shot, another, and then five or six more in quick succession [ring] out with startling distinctness over on the Mill Springs road, a mile or more to our left and front." Some of the men assumed that the pickets were skirmishing with Rebel cavalry, who had made several excursions toward the crossroads in the preceding weeks. The 10th Indiana, camped closest to the crossroads, knew better. When the firing started, the pickets sent a courier to the camp to tell their officers, including brigade commander Mahlon Manson, that the Southern army was attacking.[73]

Pickets from the 10th Indiana contend with the Confederate advance. From a wartime patriotic cover (envelope). *Courtesy of the Kentucky Historical Society.*

The courier found Manson and breathlessly sputtered the news. Manson, a Mexican War veteran, druggist, Indiana legislator and former colonel of the 10th Indiana, ordered the long roll sounded. As the regiment prepared to march, Lieutenant Colonel William C. Kise, commander of the 10th Indiana, immediately sent Major Miller and Company A to reinforce the pickets. Shortly thereafter, the remainder of the regiment, some of whom had been cooking breakfast, grabbed their equipment, fell into ranks and marched down the road at the double-quick.[74]

Manson, unused to brigade command, did not send an aide to spread word of the fight. Instead, he rode to the camp of the 4th Kentucky, which was three-fourths of a mile away. Upon his arrival, Manson woke up Colonel Speed Fry and told him to send his regiment forward. Manson's directions about where to deploy were unclear, so Fry readied his men to march toward the sound of battle. Manson then rode to the northwest, toward Thomas's headquarters.[75]

On his way to find Thomas, Manson passed the camp of the 2nd Minnesota and the 9th Ohio, part of Colonel Robert McCook's brigade. Manson told their commanders that the army was under attack. He then continued to Thomas's headquarters, located several miles away from the crossroads. Breathless from adrenaline and the ride, Manson told Thomas that his pickets had been driven in. Thomas, exasperated that Manson had personally delivered the news, interrupted Manson and said, "Damn you, sir, go back to your command and fight it." The commander then told Manson to stifle the Rebel advance and await the entire army. Manson departed, and on his way to the battleground, he again stopped to tell Kenny's and Standart's artillery batteries to prepare for action.[76]

Chapter 5

When Wesley Elmore of the 10th Indiana awoke on January 19, he prepared his breakfast in the cold rain. He quickly realized, however, that he had more to worry about than the frigid temperature. "The First we New [*sic*] of the Fight we were preparing to Eat Breakfast when our messenger came in from the scene of action and the Camp was Soon alarmed by the long Roll and we were Shortly arrayed in line of Battle with our guns and Cartridge Boxes on we were Hurried off to the Battle," Elmore wrote. Within minutes, he and his 709 comrades were rushing down the Mill Springs Road, toward the rattling musketry.[77]

Leading the way was the regiment's commander, Lieutenant Colonel William C. Kise. Born in Fayette County, Kentucky, on January 30, 1815, he moved with his family to Indianapolis and then to Hendricks County, Indiana, when Kise was a child. A Mexican War veteran, Kise was a county clerk in Boone County, Indiana, and an 1860 presidential elector for Stephen A. Douglas. When the Civil War began, Kise raised a company and was elected captain. Placed in the 10th Indiana, the unit fought at Rich Mountain, Virginia. When it was reorganized for three years' service, Kise became lieutenant colonel. At Mill Springs, he led the regiment.[78]

Members of the 10th Indiana were bound by proximity and familial devotion. Most were recruited from Indiana's eighth congressional district. In addition, according to historian Gerald Prokopowicz, at least 20 percent of the original 979 recruits were related to one another. Companies A, F and I hailed from Boone County; Company B was from Montgomery

County; companies C and K were from Clinton County; Company D from Benton, Warren and Tippecanoe counties; E and H were from Tippecanoe County; and Company G was from Fountain County. Their uniforms, "a State militia suit of light gray, with a black velvet collar and cuffs," certainly added to the confusion at Mill Springs. Therefore, just as some of the Rebel units wore blue, the Hoosiers donned light gray. They were, however, better armed than their Southern counterparts and carried Enfield rifles.[79]

While Kise prepared his men for battle, Major Miller and Company A reached the Union pickets. They found them on a hill immediately south of where a farm road intersected the Mill Springs Road from the southwest at a sixty-five-degree angle. The farm road was bordered by a tall rail fence. Upon reaching the area, Miller found Company K "falling back on Company I," which had formed a battle line on the hill. They faced south, toward an open field. Miller immediately reinforced the pickets' line by creating a three-company front of about three hundred men. Miller placed Company A on the left flank and Company K on the right, with Company I anchoring the center. As Miller ordered them to "commence firing," Kise arrived on the field with the regiment's remaining seven companies. Kise formed his men about seventy-five yards behind Miller. They deployed near the intersection of the Mill Springs Road and the farm road.[80]

As the three companies cut loose with their Enfields, Miller ran back to Kise's line, which stretched across the Mill Springs Road. Finding Kise in the fog, and fearful of friendly-fire casualties, Miller told Kise "not to fire until he came up in line with us." Kise then ordered the 10th Indiana forward to join companies A, I and K. Upon advancing, he found the three companies "hotly engaged." The Kentucky-born Hoosier placed companies F, D, C, H and E on the right side of the three companies and posted companies G and B on the left, "in an open field." Therefore, when the companies formed a battle line, they were out of their usual order. A veteran of the 1st Kentucky Cavalry, which still had some men in the fight, noted that the Hoosiers "formed across the road, the right in a woods, and the left extending into an old field." The regimental historian of the 10th Indiana remarked that Kise moved them "forward through the woods to the inner line of pickets, our left resting on the road over which the enemy was advancing, our right reaching out into the timber which here was a growth of saplings and brush." Zollicoffer's delay in waiting for his regiments gave the 10th Indiana time to rush their entire unit into the fight and to stall the Rebel advance. Although the companies were out of order, the Indianans' Enfield rifles erupted against the 15th Mississippi.[81]

While trees provided some cover, Indianan Wesley Elmore complained that the company "on the Extreme left was pushed out into an open Field contrary to our wishes." Elmore noted that after marching "through the Woods," his regiment "stoped [*sic*] Supposing we were close enough to the Yellow Coats." Soon, Kise reported, "a regiment of rebels were advancing in line of battle and their treasonable colors were seen flaunting in the breeze. The fire continued without cessation." Captain I. W. Perkins remarked that the Confederates were initially three hundred yards away, illustrating the slow pace of Zollicoffer's advance. When the skirmishers from the 15th Mississippi saw that the Federals had established a battle line with a full regiment, they fell back to their own unit. Integrating the two skirmish companies into the ranks likely caused additional delays for the 15th Mississippi.[82]

The 10th Indiana faced two Rebel regiments: the 15th Mississippi on its left, on the east side of the road, and the 19th Tennessee on its right, on the west side of the road. Therefore, the outnumbered Hoosiers were relieved when reinforcements arrived. As the Southern army readjusted its lines on the ridge three hundred yards to the south, 250 members of Colonel Frank Wolford's 1st Kentucky Cavalry rode to the scene. Dismounting, the troopers formed in the open field on the left side of the 10th Indiana. Kentuckian J. A. Brents wrote, "Here our cavalry and the Indianans stood shoulder to shoulder, and fought the entire rebel force for about one hour." This was Wolford's entire command, for his remaining companies were absent on scouting duties near Prestonsburg and Paintsville in eastern Kentucky.[83]

Wolford did not have the spit and polish of a career military man. Although he was a Mexican War veteran, he was a successful attorney whose regiment—known as the "Wild Riders"—was infamous for its lack of discipline. At Mill Springs, Wolford's appearance was far from soldierly. Tarrant wrote that "his face had been undefiled by water or razor for some time and he wore a homespun brown jeans coat, an old slouched hat and rode an old roan horse." His men, however, were ready for a fight.[84]

With the Rebel advance stalled, the 10th Indiana fixed bayonets and moved about one hundred yards toward the Confederates, presumably to find terrain that provided a better defensive position. They likely stopped on a knoll that had a ravine to their immediate right. The Hoosiers were proud that their pickets had held off the Confederates. "Our Pickets Fought them Nobly until we Filled their Places," Wesley Elmore commented. The Indiana soldiers were, however, in danger, especially as they moved closer to the enemy. "The continual 'zip,' 'zip,' of the bullets soon settled the fact that the 10th was engaged in a battle," Hoosier James Shaw wrote.[85]

Left: Union Colonel Frank Wolford, commander of the 1st Kentucky Cavalry. One of Wolford's soldiers wrote that at Mill Springs, Wolford's "face had been undefiled by water or razor for some time and he wore a homespun brown jeans coat, an old slouched hat and rode an old roan horse." Wolford's troopers fought dismounted during much of the Battle of Mill Springs. *Courtesy of the Library of Congress.*

Below: The Union lines became obscured from black powder smoke as the Federal troops fired at the advancing Confederates. From a wartime patriotic cover (envelope). *Courtesy of the Kentucky Historical Society.*

The fight gained in intensity when the 19th Tennessee, fighting on the west side of the road, advanced toward the Union right. The Tennesseans moved down the hill and past the cabin. Although the Hoosiers saw the Tennesseans advance through the fog, Kise told his men to hold their fire. The Confederates neared the Union position and shot several volleys, their buck and ball rounds crashing into the Federal ranks. Finally, Kise ordered his men to shoot. Elmore wrote, "So we commenced the work and we Kept up a Constant Fire on them." Harrison added, "We gave them a hearty welcome as they came up in sight and we gave them some of the Enfield slugs which made them weak in the knees. We stood and fought them till we was out of ammunition."[86]

The fog and black powder smoke limited the troops' line of sight. "Owing to the foggy morning," Tarrant wrote, "and the thinness of the atmosphere, the smoke of the conflict hovered down over the contestants like a pall, as if to shroud the bloody carnage." Chaplain W. H. Honnell also recalled the poor visibility: "The darkness of the morning was increased by the heavy rain and dense smoke of the battle, so that it became difficult to distinguish the battle line." Captain W. B. Carroll of the 10th Indiana simply stated, "The morning was rainy and afterwards the smoke made it difficult to see."[87]

Although visibility was poor, when the 19th Tennessee advanced, the shooting became "almost constant." More of Zollicoffer's regiments arrived and formed on the ridge immediately south of the Union position. Since Zollicoffer, the brigade commander, was with the 19th Tennessee, these new arrivals were not deployed in a timely manner. Instead of directing his entire brigade, Zollicoffer's attention was focused on the 19th Tennessee. Some regimental commanders, however, took the initiative. As the 19th Tennessee advanced on the west side of the road, the 15th Mississippi, after reintegrating its two skirmish companies, pressed forward with the 20th Tennessee behind it. The 25th Tennessee moved in on the Rebel left flank and formed in the rear of the 19th Tennessee. Manson later commented that these Confederates "exhibited a courage and determination worthy of a better cause."[88]

Several factors aided the Union defense against the multiple Rebel regiments. First, the poor roads slowed the Southern advance and prevented the Confederates from overrunning their position. Second, with Zollicoffer remaining with the 19th Tennessee, he did not direct other regiments into the action. Therefore, several Confederate units, left to their own devices, either did not deploy in a timely manner or were thrown into the action piecemeal. Third, the smoke and fog aided the Union defense because the Southerners did not know how many soldiers they faced, so they advanced with caution. Fourth, the Federals found a good, defensible position, with the line being partially covered by woods. The Southern soldiers had to advance over rough country, including several ravines. Finally, the Union soldiers' weapons were better, with their Enfield rifles being more effective than the Southern flintlocks, some of which did not fire in the rain.

These advantages did not prevent the fight from growing more intense. Samuel Patterson of the 10th Indiana remarked, "i [*sic*] got my ramrod shot [in two] while I was aloading it [which] snatched it [bald headed]." Elmore related, "I do not see How any of us Escaped their Bullets For they Fell like Hail around us But the Great God Protected us in the Right." Casualties mounted. Ebenezer Dixon was shot in the head and killed, Mike Grady was hit in the mouth and died, Oscar Shanklin was struck in the hand, a Lieutenant McAdams was shot in the forehead and killed, a Lieutenant Johnson was wounded in the arm and "Kise had his hat shot from his head."[89]

After fighting for an hour, during which time there were several pauses in the action, the Confederates massed their men against the Union position. Lieutenant Lewis Johnston of the 10th Indiana said that the Confederate "line extended five or six times as long as one regiment" and saw the "three distinct lines" of the 19th Tennessee, 15th Mississippi and 20th Tennessee move toward their position. Other Hoosiers concurred, stating that the Southerners had three times their number.[90]

The Rebels inched closer, held at bay by the Federals' rifled muskets. Kise reported, "The battle was at its hottest, and our ranks were gradually becoming thinned and mutilated." Suddenly, Rebel cavalry moved against the right flank of the 10th Indiana while the commander of the 15th Mississippi, Lieutenant Colonel Walthall, moved around the Hoosiers' left and into a deep ravine to outflank the Union position. Kise shifted Company F to the right to contest the cavalry. According to Major Miller, three companies—A, D and F—saw Rebels firing at the regiment "from a house to our right." Therefore, those companies advanced to shove the Confederates back. Kise noted that his troops "opened a galling fire," but his defensive plan crumbled. Confederate flanking fire poured in from the right as the 19th Tennessee and the cavalry moved in. Kise bent back the right side of his line to respond to the threat. With the chaos of battle and the poor visibility, the order to bend the line caused confusion.

Smoke rolls between the lines as Union and Confederate soldiers fight near a split-rail fence. From a wartime patriotic cover (envelope). *Courtesy of the Kentucky Historical Society.*

Some Hoosiers believed that a retreat had been ordered. Samuel McIlvaine wrote that "from some misunderstanding of the command, or other reason, only the right wing at first fell back and that only partially and in Indian style, loading and firing from behind trees as we went." At the same time, the 15th Mississippi outflanked the Federals and fired into their left. The two Indiana companies on that side responded, Elmore wrote, noting that "it was time for us to do Some Execution."[91]

Just as the Confederates were slow in deploying their troops, so, too, were the Federals. Reinforcements were not sent in a timely manner. With confusion in the ranks, ammunition running low, Rebel troops outflanking the line and no reinforcements visible in the thick woods behind them, the Union troops fell back to the north. Part of the confusion resulted from the 10th Indiana's companies being out of order. "After fighting there a good while the enemy [the 15th Mississippi] had got round on the left of us," Miller testified. "They [the 19th Tennessee] also had a line in front of us." Therefore, he noted, "the order came to fall back or we would be surrounded." According to Lieutenant Johnston, they fell back slowly, in a line of battle, while Miller added that they "fell back in as good order as the nature of the ground would [permit], as the woods being very thick." Upon seeing the Federals withdraw, the Confederates cheered and pressed

Looking into the ravine on the east side of the road from the Union position along the farm road. Confederate troops attacked out of the ravine and toward this position, a split-rail fence that separated the road from a field. *Courtesy of the author.*

forward, the 19th Tennessee moving up on the right side of the road and the 15th Mississippi continuing their flanking movement into the ravine. Although the 1st Kentucky deployed, Wolford reported, into "the head of the hollow" and initially slowed the Mississippians, the Kentuckians fell back when the Hoosiers departed. Honnell remarked that they left "the open grounds covered by our dead."[92]

With the yip of the Rebel yell filling the woods and ravines south of Logan's Crossroads, the Federals withdrew, Honnell wrote, "in good order to the west fence of Logan's field." This fence, which ran along the farm road that cut into the Mill Springs Road at a sixty-five-degree angle, faced a steep ravine that ran nearly parallel to the Mill Springs Road. Knowing that the 15th Mississippi was pressing into the ravine, the 1st Kentucky formed behind the fence and faced east, Tarrant remarked, "thus forming a right angle with the [10th Indiana] regiment," which was positioned across the Mill Springs Road, facing southward toward the 19th Tennessee. With this position, Miller testified, the Hoosiers formed in "the edge of the woods to the old field in front of our camp." Therefore, the Union line was bent, with the 1st Kentucky along the fence on the left flank facing southeast toward the ravine and the 10th Indiana across the Mill Springs Road in the edge of some woods, facing southward. To their relief, and after an hour of fighting, additional reinforcements arrived.[93]

The Union withdrawal must have been rapid, for Company F of the 10th Indiana was left behind. Posted on the extreme right, the company had bent its line "at right angles" to meet the Confederate cavalry. Just as the 15th Mississippi pressed into a ravine on the east side of the road and used terrain to their advantage, the Rebel cavalry facing Company F on the west side of the lane also entered a hollow. Hoosier captain Benjamin Gregory said that the Rebel horsemen were "behind a hill in the ravine." His company did not hear the order to fall back, so they were left alone when the Federals withdrew. Gregory's men fired at the cavalry, who remained in the ravine peppering the Indianans with gunfire. "They fired at us almost constantly," Gregory remarked. In this "severe contest," he lost three killed and seven wounded, with one of the injured men later dying. In testimony that details the many lulls in the battle, as well as the Confederates' inability to mass their troops, Gregory noted that his unsupported company fought the cavalry for approximately twenty minutes before they withdrew, firing as they pulled back to their regiment. When Company F reached the newly established Federal line, the men were nearly out of ammunition. During the battle, some members of the regiment fired sixty to seventy-five rounds.[94]

After the battle, controversy erupted over claims that the 10th Indiana had fought alone for nearly an hour. Some officers in other regiments denied the Hoosiers' role during the opening phases of the battle, but evidence dictates that they fought with part of the 1st Kentucky Cavalry for that amount of time. After the war, Kise indignantly noted that Thomas's official report did not highlight the regiment's role against the Rebel vanguard. This report, Kise claimed, ignored the first hour of the fight because Thomas disliked Manson, the Hoosiers' brigade commander. In addition, Thomas probably failed to note the first hour because it reflected poorly on officers who did not deploy reinforcements in a timely manner. This included Thomas, who did not arrive on the field until at least an hour had passed. After the battle, Kise was court-martialed for supposedly falsifying his after-action report. In the testimony from that proceeding, and in letters written immediately after the battle, many soldiers state that the regiment fought alone for forty-five minutes to one hour.[95]

Since Mill Springs was fought early in the war and some soldiers envisioned a quick end to the conflict, several officers downplayed the participation of other regiments so that their troops could claim the glory. These officers discounted the Hoosiers' role—and the part played by the 1st Kentucky—in slowing the Confederate advance and bearing the brunt of the initial attack. One member of the 2nd Minnesota, for example, called the 1st Kentucky "the first and best runners of the day...they did not fight well." He added that the 10th Indiana was also worthless, stating, "The men had a hard position, and did as well as they could while distracted by such diverse and bewildering orders of mad, hair-brained [*sic*] officers." The 10th Indiana, however, lost more men than any other Union regiment in the battle, with most of these casualties incurred during the first hour of the fight.[96]

Chapter 6

The 4th Kentucky Infantry Regiment was posted in a thick wood, bivouacked a half mile behind the camp of the 10th Indiana. When the Confederates hit the Hoosier pickets, their brigade commander, Mahlon Manson, cut through the Kentuckians' camp while on his way to tell Thomas about the enemy attack. Manson woke up Colonel Speed Fry and, in a vague order, told Fry to move to the fight. Upon Manson's return from Thomas's headquarters, Manson found Fry's regiment "in the road leading to my camp." Manson told Fry to hurry forward and "take a position in the woods." Fry's unit, however, did not reach the 10th Indiana until nearly an hour had passed. When they did move forward, Fry noted, his regiment and Kenny's battery advanced to the sound of the fighting.[97]

Fry was not a professional soldier, but he did have military experience. Born on September 9, 1817, near Danville, Kentucky, Fry was the eighth of thirteen children born to Thomas Walker and Elizabeth Smith Fry. His grandfather, an early settler to the area, had been a prominent local teacher whose students included Kentucky politician Joshua Fry Bell and the noted emancipationist Cassius Marcellus Clay. Speed attended local schools, including Danville's Centre College, before graduating from Wabash College in Crawfordsville, Indiana. He then studied law under an uncle, was licensed in 1843 and opened a practice in Danville. Unhappy as an attorney, Fry opened a mercantile business. When the Mexican War erupted, he raised a company of volunteers. Their flag, made by Danville's First Presbyterian Church Sunday school, was inscribed "Speed S. Fry—Conquer or Die." Fry became captain of Company B of the 2nd Kentucky Infantry, and the regiment fought at Buena Vista, where Fry distinguished himself. The 2nd Kentucky served for a year, mustering out in New Orleans in June 1847.[98]

Union Colonel Speed Fry, a native of Danville, Kentucky, led the 4th Kentucky Infantry at Mill Springs. Fry was given credit for killing Confederate General Felix Zollicoffer and later became a brigadier general. *Courtesy of the Library of Congress.*

Upon his return to Danville, Fry resumed his business affairs. In 1851, he ran for Boyle County judge (county administrator) as a Whig and was elected for two four-year terms. With the outbreak of the Civil War, Fry organized the Boyle County Home Guard and enlisted one hundred men in April 1861. After helping deliver "Lincoln guns" to Unionists in the region, Fry took his men to Camp Dick Robinson, where they joined the 4th Kentucky. On October 9, 1861, the regiment was mustered in, and Fry was elected colonel. He stood five feet, nine inches tall, wore a thick beard and was described by one member of the 2nd Minnesota as "as brave a man as ever lived."[99]

Fry's 4th Kentucky was one of the first Union regiments raised in the state. The troops hailed from Boyle, Mercer, Anderson, Washington, Rockcastle, Laurel, Estill, Montgomery, Rowan, Lewis, Bourbon, Nicholas, Pendleton, Harrison and Grant counties. At least one-fifth of the men were from Boyle County, and at least sixteen of the officers came from Danville. Armed with Enfield rifles, the troops joined Thomas's command at Lebanon. By the time they arrived at Logan's Crossroads, the ranks had been depleted by sickness. Although the unit initially had more than eight hundred men, it went into

Downtown Danville, the county seat of Boyle County, Kentucky. At least one-fifth of the soldiers in the 4th Kentucky (Union) Infantry were from Boyle County, and at least sixteen of the officers came from Danville. *Courtesy of Centre College.*

the fight with four hundred troops and only half of its company officers. The healthy ones were prepared for the fight, however, for many marched toward the battle with seventy rounds of ammunition.[100]

Fry led the 4th Kentucky southward where they met the 10th Indiana and 1st Kentucky Cavalry at the farm road that intersected the Mill Springs Road. When Fry's troops arrived, the Hoosiers were low on ammunition. The 19th Tennessee, west of the road, was firing at the 10th Indiana, while the 15th Mississippi was moving into the ravine east of the Union position. This flanking move may have been ordered by Crittenden, who arrived on the field at 7:30 a.m. and directed Zollicoffer to lengthen his line to outflank the Federals. The more likely case is that the Mississippi officers moved in that direction on their own during one of the many lulls in the fighting. The Confederates had not reconnoitered the battlefield, so the Mississippians were probably unaware that the ravine was deep. To assault the Union left, they had to march over rough terrain before moving eastward up a steep hill. In many instances, the troops could not see one another from the ravine, a plight that added to the confusion of the fight.[101]

Because of the fog, the Mississippians used landmarks to guide their regiment. After marching northeast to outflank the Union line, the Confederates lined up at a blacksmith's shop on the eastern rim of the hollow. They then marched westward toward the Union troops who were posted along the split-rail fence at the farm road.

When the 4th Kentucky arrived, portions of the 10th Indiana and the 1st Kentucky fell back toward their camps. For them, the reinforcements signaled that their work was done. Kise wrote that while two-thirds of the 10th Indiana returned to camp, the remaining one-third stayed near the Mill Springs Road fighting while the 4th Kentucky formed on their left. As the Kentuckians deployed, Captain J. A. Vaughan of the 4th Kentucky recalled, Fry was "riding an iron-gray horse. He wore a blue military cap, a single-breasted blue uniform coat, with colonel's shoulder straps." Vaughan also described how the Kentuckians "left the road and turned into an open field up the ridge, still marching by the right flank, along a line of worm fence, back of which was heavy timber, underbrush, and the road we had left." Seeing the Confederates in the ravine, the 4th Kentucky faced the hollow. Their left flank stretched downhill behind the fence along the farm road, and their right flank rose uphill toward the Mill Springs Road. The remnants of the 10th Indiana stayed on the right flank of the 4th Kentucky, which was posted in a field on the west side of the road. A number of Wolford's cavalry remained on the left of the 4th Kentucky. J. A. Brents wrote that the line was "resting behind the fence and in a skirt of timber."[102]

Unionist R. M. Kelly described the position: "A ravine ran through the open field parallel to Fry's front, heading near the road on his right, with steep sides in his front, but sloping gradually beyond his left." Fry had a good position, with another veteran remarking that "the battleground was in the form of a triangle; an old field on one side and a dense wood on the other, with a County road between the old field and the woods." Kise wrote that when Fry's men appeared, they "opened a deadly fire on the ranks of the enemy." With these reinforcements, Kise "rallied the right wing" and stabilized the remnants of his line.[103]

After the 15th Mississippi pressed into the ravine, the 20th Tennessee, which had followed the Mississippians, formed on the east rim of the hollow, near the blacksmith shop. The regiment was commanded by the aptly named Colonel Joel Battle, a Seminole War veteran and native of Davidson County, Tennessee. Battle had been a state legislator and a general in the Tennessee State Militia. In April 1861, he raised a company and became colonel of the 20th Tennessee. He fought at Barbourville, and at Mill Springs, his son, Joel Battle Jr., was seriously wounded. Sadly, three months after Mill Springs, two of Battle's sons were killed at the Battle of Shiloh. Battle was captured while trying to recover the body of one of them. At Mill Springs, Battle conspicuously led his troops. In one instance, when his men were advancing, Union musketry raked the line. "Don't dodge, men, don't dodge!" Battle exhorted. Immediately, an artillery shell roared by, and Battle ducked. The men laughed, and Battle shouted, "Boys, dodge the big ones, but don't dodge the little ones!"[104]

Battle's regiment soon faced the 4th Kentucky. Fry reported that when he moved into position, his troops did so "under a heavy and galling fire from the enemy, who were concealed in a deep ravine at the foot of the hill [the 15th Mississippi] and posted on the opposite hill, distant about 250 yards [the 20th Tennessee]." After the war, Fry added, "No sooner was the line formed than a heavy fire was opened upon us from this ravine and a dense thicket just beyond." The fog continued to be problematic. Vaughan remarked that "we could not see the enemy in person at first, but fired at the gun-flashes."[105]

Because of the poor visibility, Confederate troops worried about friendly-fire casualties. Once, when Walthall led the 15th Mississippi forward, his skirmishers reported that the 20th Tennessee was to their front. Walthall told his men to lie down while he and a lieutenant moved forward to scout

A view from the eastern rim of the ravine, looking toward the Union position along the farm road. The 15th Mississippi and 20th Tennessee attacked out of this ravine. The difficult terrain helped dismantle unit cohesion at Mill Springs. *Courtesy of the author.*

out the mystery regiment. Upon finding them, Walthall shouted, "What troops are those?" The reply was "Kentucky." Because of the fog and the Rebels' inconsistent uniforms, Crittenden had directed that the password "Kentucky" be used to identify friendly troops. To ensure that he had heard the correct password, Walthall yelled, "Who *are* you?" Again, the response was "Kentucky." Thinking that this was a friendly regiment, Walthall ordered one of his flags unfurled. Immediately, the Unionist Kentuckians—to whom Walthall had been speaking—fired a volley of musketry. The banner was riddled with bullets, the flagstaff cut in two and the lieutenant killed. Walthall returned to the regiment and exclaimed, "Now I think you know who they are!"[106]

Upon his arrival at the fence, Fry's exuberance got the better of him. Unable to clearly see the Confederates in the ravine, the Kentucky colonel pushed the 4th Kentucky across the fence and into the open field that sloped into the hollow. With the exception of some scrub growth, the field and the ravine were open where the blacksmith had cleared the area to fuel his forge. When the Kentuckians left their cover, the Mississippians advanced up the ridge. Fry realized his mistake, reporting that the "engagement at once became very warm." He then ordered his men back to the fence, with "the enemy continuing to fire upon us all the while." Vaughan recalled that "it got too hot for us and we fell back behind the fence into the underbrush."[107]

The Confederates mistakenly believed that Fry's withdrawal was a retreat. Supposing that the Kentuckians were panicked, the Mississippians rushed up the hill. The 4th Kentucky, however, turned and faced the Rebels, holding their fire until, Fry explained, "they got almost in bayonet reach of our guns." The Federal muskets erupted, "which not only surprised" the enemy "but at once checked their advance." The Kentuckians returned to the fence, and the Mississippians withdrew into the ravine, where they prepared for another charge.[108]

To strike the Union position, the poorly trained and inadequately armed Confederates had to maneuver through forests and underbrush while keeping their battle lines intact. The troops' inexperience and the broken terrain ruined unit cohesion, caused delays and continually led to piecemeal attacks. In addition, the rough ground and lack of visibility prevented the Rebels from adequately using their artillery. In fact, the Federals were surprised by these disorganized assaults. One remarked that the Rebels "were not in fair-battle order, but swarmed in the woods like Indians, though keeping in line and whooping like savages." Discrepancies in dress and weaponry also confounded the Northerners. "The rebel soldiers were not generally clothed in uniform, but in citizens' clothes," a soldier wrote. "Their weapons were mixed—squirrel rifles, &c...I have seen all kinds of weapons."[109]

With frequent pauses in the fighting and the Rebels' use of the ravine to maneuver and find cover, Fry lost his patience. The Kentuckian jumped on the fence, shook his fist at the Rebels and yelled at them to advance. According to R. M. Kelly, Fry "in stentorian tones denounced them as dastards and defied them to stand up on their feet and come forward like men." Fry did not have to wait long. The Southerners closed on Fry's position, charging up the hill through the smoke at least two more times, "with bayonets fixed and their large cane-knives unsheathed." The Confederates were again driven back. One Federal soldier wrote, "Our bullets were sent with unerring aim—many rebels shot in the forehead, breast, and stomach."[110]

The 20th Tennessee followed the 15th Mississippi into the fight, moving down into the ravine from the blacksmith's shop. The terrain and the fog slowed Battle's deployment, and the officer moved his regiment to the right of the 15th Mississippi to strike the extreme left of the Federal line. Because of the terrain, the Unionists on the hill sometimes overshot the Mississippians and poured bullets into the 20th Tennessee.[111]

Battle's regiment moved out of the ravine, pressing behind and to the right of the 15th Mississippi. Part of the 20th Tennessee struck Wolford's dismounted Kentucky cavalry, posted in a cornfield on the far left of the Union line. The Kentuckians put up a stubborn defense. One Tennessean remarked, "We were in the battle under a terrific fire." Their regimental flag was struck multiple times and the flagstaff broken. Joel Battle Jr. was "badly wounded" when he grabbed the colors. In addition, Second Lieutenant R. D. Anderson was wounded three times, his clothes were pierced seven times and his sword scabbard was "shot in two." Private Shelton Crosthwaite of Rutherford County, Tennessee, who was arguably "the most intellectual as well as the best informed man in the Company," was injured. Despite his wound, Crosthwaite continued fighting, saying, "Boys, they have shot me, but I can still shoot." Shortly thereafter, Crosthwaite was killed. Fry noted that some of the fighting took place at "ten paces," and one member of the 20th Tennessee wrote that "some of the men reached the fence and the slaughter was simply terrible."[112]

"This was our first regular battle," another Tennessean explained, "and our company and regiment had suffered dreadfully; it was reported afterwards that…we had lost forty percent of the number engaged." The 4th Kentucky ran low on ammunition and fixed bayonets. Below them, confusion reigned among some of the Southern officers. One Rebel wrote, "At first, and for nearly two hours, the tide of battle was in our favor; but at this time no one seemed to have command." With Zollicoffer several hundred yards away with the 19th Tennessee, few officers took charge. Furthermore, the Union musketry was terrific. "For two hours the bullets fell all around me," one Confederate wrote, "and sometimes passed within a few inches of my head, if I may judge from the whistling noise they made."[113]

The amount of gunfire was evident to those who toured the area after the fight. One correspondent wrote that "the severity of the fighting may be reckoned from the fact that in places the underbrush, with which the woods were filled, was cut down by the storm of balls. There were thickets in which not a stick could be discovered that was not shattered by balls." A Union soldier concurred: "Trees were flecked with bullets, underbrush cut away as with a scythe. Dead and wounded lay along the fence, on the one side the Blue on the other the Gray; enemy dead were everywhere scattered across the open field."[114]

Most of this damage was caused by bullets, not artillery fire. While infantrymen clawed through smoke-filled ravines, few cannons were deployed because of the rough terrain and poor visibility. When Zollicoffer's brigade advanced, two guns of Captain A. M. Rutledge's battery were posted on a ridge east of the cabin where the 10th Indiana's pickets had stalled the Rebel advance. Because Rutledge's battery could not see any targets, they fired only a few rounds. Furthermore, Rutledge's horse was shot out from under him, which dampened the officer's ardor. The cannons withdrew after a short time. Crittenden explained that, "owing to the formation and character of the field of battle, I was unable to use my artillery and cavalry to advantage in the action." Echoing this sentiment, R. M. Kelly wrote that "there was little opportunity for the effective use of artillery on either side, and that arm played an insignificant part in the engagement." Standart's battery, for example, had difficulty deploying and fired only twenty times. Other batteries, however, took part whether or not they could see the enemy. Union Captain Henry Wetmore's battery, for example, engaged in indirect fire at the Rebel cannons. Artilleryman Joseph Durfee wrote that "for about an hour we had to fire over the woods in the direction of the enemy's artillery, the roar of which was all we had to direct us. We fired our shells in earnest." Their fire was sometimes lethal. According to Durfee, "one of them struck a [stump], and, bursting, killed 10 and wounded 8" Confederates. The Rebel guns were ineffective, prompting Colonel Robert McCook to report that the Confederate cannons "constantly overshot my brigade." Despite the artillery's overall ineffectiveness, the cannons bolstered the confidence of one Union soldier. He wrote that the Federal guns "seemed to be of immense use to us." Although artillery did not significantly impact the battle, their sound uplifted the troops' morale.[115]

Captain Dennis Kenny's section of the 1st Ohio Light Artillery provides a good example of how artillery was used at Mill Springs. When the 4th Kentucky was fighting the 15th Mississippi, Kenny's guns moved forward "through the timber by a narrow angling road" and stopped in "the open field where the battle appeared to be heaviest." The artillery halted in the cornfield to the left and rear of the 4th Kentucky, unlimbering behind the 1st Kentucky Cavalry. They fired seven shells into the ravine but pulled back when the 20th Tennessee advanced. Because of the hilly terrain, clear shots were difficult, negating the guns' overall effectiveness. In addition, the Rebels used the hollow to maneuver under cover. When the Southerners finally made an inviting target, they were too close for comfort, and the battery withdrew.[116]

The rough terrain prevented both sides from effectively deploying their artillery. This image from a wartime patriotic cover (envelope) shows a Union artillery battery moving into position. *Courtesy of the Kentucky Historical Society.*

Just as the Confederate artillery was ineffective, the rain rendered many of the Rebels' flintlock muskets equally worthless. James L. Cooper of the 20th Tennessee wrote, "We rushed up to the 15th Mississippi with only a fence between us and the enemy and did the best we could with our old flintlocks." Several factors hindered the weapons' performance. First, the Confederates' smoothbore muskets had limited range. While the Federals were armed with rifled muskets that were effective up to three hundred yards, the Southern smoothbores could shoot only up to one hundred yards. Therefore, when the 17th Tennessee fired from two hundred yards, "the balls fell harmlessly short." Second, the rain made many of the flintlocks useless because the weapons had to be primed on the outside with black powder. If the pan for the priming powder became wet, the powder would not ignite and the gun would not fire. Multiple sources contend that the rain made many flintlocks ineffective at Mill Springs, but exact numbers are difficult to ascertain. Cooper believed that "not one in three" would shoot. "Mine went off once in the action," he wrote, "and although I wiped the 'pan' and primed a dozen times it would do so no more." Other estimates contend that one in five of the muskets would not shoot, while Carroll wrote that half of the Rebel guns were useless. More conservative estimates hold that one in ten of the guns would not fire. Bill Neikirk, former president of the Mill Springs Battlefield Association, argues that more of the flintlocks fired than the Confederates readily admitted. Neikirk, who has done archaeological investigations on the field to locate battle lines, notes that thousands of smoothbore musket balls have been found on the battlefield. Therefore, archaeological evidence points to the more conservative estimate. While a large number of the Rebel guns certainly did not fire, the exact number was probably exaggerated by Confederate officers in order to provide an additional excuse for why their army failed at Mill Springs.[117]

For the soldiers whose lives were put in danger by faulty flintlocks, frustrations were evident. One member of the 19th Tennessee "saw two or three of the boys break their guns over the fence, after several attempts to fire them." In the 20th Tennessee, some of the troops who tried to shoot as many as six times smashed the useless muskets on trees. The regiments most affected appear to have been the 17th, 19th and 20th Tennessee Infantry regiments, and some of these troops were allowed to go to the rear. As Crittenden explained, "It rained violently throughout the action, rendering all the flint-lock guns useless. The men bearing them were allowed to fall back on the reserve."[118]

After the war, Jefferson Davis commented on the episode in his book, *The Rise and Fall of the Confederate Government*. Davis noted, "The heart of even a noble enemy must be moved at the spectacle of citizens defending their homes, with muskets of obsolete patterns and shot-guns, against an invader having all the modern improvements in arms." Assuredly, the antiquated guns led to more Confederate casualties and influenced the outcome of the battle. In addition, the flintlocks' failure to fire probably caused many of the lulls that occurred during the fight. Pauses in the action happened because soldiers had to interrupt their respective charges in order to wipe the rain from the pan of their guns before priming them. One member of the 20th Tennessee concluded that if the weather had "been fair, or had we been armed with percussion [cap] guns, the result of that battle would have been far different. It rained nearly all the time and our 'Flint Locks' would not fire. Our men lost much time in drawing loads from their guns, the powder having gotten wet in the rain. Many of them never fired a dozen shots."[119]

Poor weapons gave Crittenden a valid excuse for why his troops did not overwhelm the Federal defenders. Since Confederate officers—notably men in Carroll's brigade—had been complaining about their lack of adequate firearms in the months preceding Mill Springs, Southern authorities were aware of the discrepancy in arms between Union and Confederate soldiers. Antiquated flintlocks did play an important role in the battle, but Crittenden's lack of leadership and the Confederates' failure to push multiple regiments against the 10th Indiana early in the action played an equal if not greater part in the Rebels' ultimate loss. While poor weapons certainly hindered the Confederates' efforts, a lack of initiative, poor leadership and piecemeal deployments were additional deciding factors.

Chapter 7

The battle had raged for approximately three hours. On the Confederate right flank, the 15th Mississippi and the 20th Tennessee vainly tried to advance out of the ravine to dislodge the 4th Kentucky Infantry and the 1st Kentucky Cavalry, who were behind the rail fence and in the cornfield. On the Rebel left flank, Zollicoffer led the 19th Tennessee though the woods and the shallower ravine where the Confederate cavalry had tried to push the stubborn remnants of the 10th Indiana back. Rain pattered down as the smoke clung to the ground. Frequent lulls, in many instances caused by the troops' inability to see one another, stopped the fighting as Rebel regiments attacked, were repulsed and then backed off in order to wipe the rain from their flintlocks. Sometimes regiments simply fired at one another from long range, aiming through the mist at the flash of enemy muskets.

When the 15th Mississippi and the 20th Tennessee entered the ravine east of the road to outflank the Union position, a wide gap opened between them and the 19th Tennessee, which fought to their left on the west side of the Mill Springs Road. During a pause in the action, Zollicoffer realized that he had lost track of the two regiments on the east side of the road. Instead of sending an aide to find the 15th Mississippi and the 20th Tennessee, Zollicoffer rode away from the 19th Tennessee and toward the road. The "dense mist of the rainy morning" still clung to the ground as the Tennessean spurred his horse forward.

Colonel David Cummings described how Zollicoffer's reconnaissance caused a pause in the fight. "The Smoke had become So dense that I could not See the enemy and I did not wish to wast [*sic*] amunition [*sic*] and a Smal force Soon Showed them selves to our right about one hundred yards distant," Cummings wrote. Although this was actually the 4th Kentucky, Cummings thought it "was the left of the 15th Miss. Supporting." He added that "they had got that far in advance whilst we had halted and when the Smoke was So dense, I could not See them at this moment. Gen. Zollicoffer road [*sic*] by me in the rear of the 19th Tenn. Reg. and being under the impression we were firing upon [them]...He ordered me to cease firing and I called upon them three times to cease firing!! Gen. Zollicoffer road behind enemy lines." Through the smoke, Cummings and Zollicoffer spotted a regiment off to the right that they believed to be the 15th Mississippi. Concerned that the regiment had gone too far forward and would be outflanked by the 10th Indiana, which was in front of the 19th Tennessee, Zollicoffer rode ahead to ensure the proper placement of that regiment. According to one Rebel staff officer, Zollicoffer also worried that this was a Confederate regiment that was firing on another Southern unit. The officer wrote that Zollicoffer's staff urged the general to stay, fearing he would be killed. Cummings and Zollicoffer, however, did not realize that the regiment one hundred yards off to their right was the 4th Kentucky.[120]

In a twist of fate, at the same time that Zollicoffer rode toward the lane, Lieutenant Colonel John Croxton of the 4th Kentucky told Fry that the Confederates were advancing through the woods to their right, moving up to where the 10th Indiana had been posted by the Mill Springs Road. Therefore, as Zollicoffer moved to his right, Fry rode to his right, toward the same location. Fry had just stood on the fence and cursed the Confederate soldiers in the ravine. During a lull that developed afterward, Fry mounted his horse and rode down the farm road to where it intersected the Mill Springs Road. There, he hoped to check his right flank to see if the Confederates were moving against that side of his line.[121]

"As I neared the road I saw an officer riding slowly down the road on a white horse, and within twenty paces of my regiment," Fry later said. "His uniform was concealed—except the extremity of his pantaloons, which I discovered were the color worn by Federal officers—by a long gum overcoat." Regiments from McCook's brigade and Carter's brigade were nearing the field. Therefore, Fry assumed that the officer—who proved to be Zollicoffer—belonged to one of those units. "His near approach to my regiment, his calm manner, my close proximity to him, indeed everything I saw led me to believe he was a Federal officer belonging to some of the regiments just arriving," Fry remarked. Since some of Carter's regiments had arrived at Logan's Crossroads shortly before the battle, there were several officers whom Fry had not met. Zollicoffer, Fry contended, could have been one of those officers. Vaughan noted that the Confederate general was wearing "a white rubber coat and a blue army cap," and some of the men in the regiment believed that he was Wolford. The lack of Southern troops near Zollicoffer reinforced the idea that he was a Union officer.[122]

Although Zollicoffer's "oil cloth overcoat" concealed his identity, Fry never understood how the Confederate did not recognize Fry as a Federal officer. "I had on nothing to conceal my uniform," Fry later remarked. Perhaps Zollicoffer's nearsightedness, coupled with the rain and fog and adrenaline of battle, prevented the Southern officer from realizing that Fry was an enemy. Regardless of the reason, Fry rode to Zollicoffer, with "our horses' heads coming very near together." The two officers met a few dozen paces south of where the farm road joined the Mill Springs Road. There was little room to move in the narrow lane, and, Fry said, he reached Zollicoffer's "side so closely that our knees touched. He was calm, self-possessed and dignified in manner."[123]

Squinting toward Fry's battle line, Zollicoffer told Fry, "We must not shoot our own men." Fry responded, "Of course not. I would not shoot our own men intentionally." Zollicoffer then pointed to his left, toward the 19th Tennessee. "Those are our men," he said. Fry peered through the smoke in that direction. Since he could not see the regiment that Zollicoffer was pointing toward, Fry rode "some fifteen or twenty paces" to his right. Looking down the road, Fry saw a staff officer ride out from behind a tree. This time, there was no mistaking that the mounted soldier was the enemy. He fired a pistol at Fry, and the bullet struck Fry's horse near the left hip. "I immediately drew my Colt's revolver from the holster," Fry wrote, but the officer rode back behind the tree. Since Zollicoffer had ridden from that direction, Fry now knew that the mysterious officer was a Confederate. Additional sources note that the staff officer also yelled, "It's the enemy, general!"[124]

Fry immediately concluded that the officer in the white gum coat had duped him. "In an instant the thought flashed across my mind that the officer with whom I had met and conversed had attempted to draw me into the snare of death or secure my capture by a false representation of his position, and, feeling thus, I aimed at him and fired." Vaughan stated that Fry said, "That is your game, is it?" and then raised his revolver. "He was standing precisely in the position in which I had left him, with his face toward me," Fry recalled. "I raised my pistol and fired. His horse turned and

Images like this one helped anoint Union Colonel Speed Fry as the killer of Confederate General Felix Zollicoffer. Fry later said of the shooting, "I raised my pistol and fired. His horse turned and he fell." *Courtesy of the Kentucky Historical Society.*

he fell, within five feet of where he had stood, upon the right of the road and at right angles to it." Tarrant noted that Fry yelled, "Shoot him!" and several Union soldiers let loose a volley. The forty-nine-year-old Zollicoffer was struck multiple times and fell dead in the road, approximately thirty to thirty-five "paces" from the right flank of the 4th Kentucky Infantry.[125]

Although eyewitness accounts of what happened to Zollicoffer differed, it is likely that the Rebel general was struck by one pistol shot, fired by Fry, and two Enfield rounds from the 4th Kentucky. In his after-action report, Manson noted that Zollicoffer was shot three times. Honnell of the 1st Kentucky Cavalry concurred but claimed that in addition to Fry's pistol shot, the 1st Kentucky Cavalry fired the other bullets. Although Fry was given credit for slaying Zollicoffer, the fatal shot likely came from one of the Enfield rounds. In 1870, however, Fry maintained that he had fired the fatal shot. "The surgeon who examined the wound informed me that the ball by which [the mortal wound] was inflicted was a minie ball," Fry recalled. I had cleaned and loaded my pistols (navy [*sic*] revolvers) with minie balls the previous morning. He also informed me that the wound was in the left breast, passing

Another romanticized image of Fry shooting Zollicoffer. *Courtesy of the Kentucky Historical Society.*

through the top of the heart." Fry added that the surgeon described the other wounds as being "not at all serious." In the same interview, Fry claimed that he had not called for the soldiers to fire. Instead, he recalled, they told him to not shoot because they believed that Zollicoffer was a Federal officer.[126]

Officers and soldiers immediately reported that Fry had killed Zollicoffer. Although Zollicoffer was cut down in a hail of musketry, the tale of a shootout between officers—albeit a one-sided shootout—made a much more compelling story. Soldiers wrote to family members and newspapers reporting the news, and Thomas's official report claimed that Fry killed the general. Four days after the battle, John Dow of the 31st Ohio informed his family that Fry was the shooter, while Wesley Elmore of the 10th Indiana wrote home that "Col Fry Killed their General Zolicofer [*sic*]." After the war, multiple regimental histories repeated the story.[127]

Some tales, however, countered the narrative. One member of the 10th Indiana claimed that Corporal James Swan, "a dead shot," fired the fatal bullet. This, however, is unlikely, considering the location of the Hoosier regiment and the lack of corroborating evidence. In a similar vein, members of the 1st Kentucky Cavalry claimed that horseman C. C. Zachary or cavalryman George Cabel killed the Rebel. Again, because of the proximity of the 4th Kentucky to Zollicoffer, these tales are also unlikely. In 1870, and again in 1900, stories appeared that a member of the 4th Kentucky named Chrisman killed Zollicoffer. It was reported that Chrisman had immense guilt about the shooting because he believed that he could have taken the general prisoner. Instead, the papers relate, Chrisman shot Zollicoffer down. The journalists added that in 1870, Chrisman "went crazy on the account of the murder" and was confined in a lunatic asylum in Hopkinsville.[128]

Although Fry probably did not fire the fatal shot, he did get credit for the killing. During and after the war, Fry either took or denied credit as it suited him. After the fight, Fry told Colonel John Marshall Harlan of the 10th Kentucky that he had shot Zollicoffer. In addition, I. B. Webster of Harlan's regiment found Fry the day after the battle and asked about the general's death. Webster said that Fry "was loth [*sic*] to talk about it" but eventually explained how it happened. Fry also told the story to at least one Confederate officer. At the Battle of Perryville, fought in October 1862, Rebel Captain James I. Hall was wounded. Taken to Danville to convalesce at the home of a prominent citizen, Hall met Fry and heard the tale. Among friends in Danville, Fry spun the story, explaining that two groups of soldiers simply stumbled into each other and started shooting. It was a misfortune of war, without any conversation on horseback. Hall later wrote:

> *As he* [General Fry] *and his staff were ascending a steep hill in a heavy rain, on nearing the summit, they discovered a party of Confederate officers ascending the opposite slope. Both parties, on account of the rain, were wearing waterproof coats which concealed completely their badges of rank. On account of the abruptness of the ascent on both sides of the hill, neither party was aware of the approach of the other until they were within buckshot range…Both parties immediately began firing with the result that General Zollicoffer was killed by a bullet from General Fry's*

> *pistol. General Fry expressed great regret at the occurrence on account of his high regard personally for General Zollicoffer.*[129]

Dr. Jefferson J. Polk, a Perryville doctor who knew Fry, recalled that "in conversation, Gen. Fry never refers to the circumstance [of Zollicoffer's death]; but I have no doubt his kind heart regrets the necessity of the event, although it happened in honorable warfare." Since some stated that Fry had shot Zollicoffer in cold blood, and since others believed that it was ungentlemanly for one officer to shoot another, Polk qualified the shooting as being "honorable." In fact, Fry's father was unimpressed with the action. Historian Richard C. Brown incorrectly noted that "Fry never publicly claimed that his bullet killed Zollicoffer" but added that Fry "never denied that it did even when he and his father, Thomas Walker Fry, became estranged because the elder Fry thought high-ranking officers should honor a code of chivalry that forbade shooting each other, especially in the back." The strained familial relationship may have caused Fry to alter the story, depending on his audience. Regardless, the *Louisville Journal* summarized the situation best by noting that "Fry, the hero of Mill Springs, [is] henceforth associated forever in American history with the misguided Zollicoffer."[130]

Zollicoffer's corpse immediately became a battlefield curiosity. Fry said that the Union soldiers did not realize that it was Zollicoffer lying in the road, but troops soon recognized him. Although Fry claimed he did not know Zollicoffer, Dr. Edward Richardson of the 12th Kentucky arrived shortly after the general's death. "I reached the body of Zollicoffer a few minutes after he fell," Richardson wrote, "the spot not being more than twenty feet in front of our line. He was quite dead...His body was penetrated by several pistol balls from the rear, and by a minnie [*sic*] ball which went clear through, from side to side. I have the General's gum coat now, and would like to send it to some of his family."[131]

Another Union officer who had been in Congress with Zollicoffer also saw the corpse. He wrote, "His face bore no expression such as is usually found upon those who fall in battle—no malice, no reckless hate, not even a shadow of physical pain. It was calm, placid, noble. I never looked upon a countenance so marked with sadness. A deep dejection had settled upon it. The low [corners] of the mouth were distinct in the droop at the corners, and the thin cheeks showed the wasting which comes through disappointment and trouble." Another Unionist correspondent recognized no nobility. "He lay by the side of the road along which we all passed," he remarked, "and

This patriotic cover (envelope) depicts Fry shooting Zollicoffer. A soldier from the 4th Kentucky saw Zollicoffer's corpse: "He had upon his person a white rubber overcoat, unbuttoned, a blue Federal army cap, and a double-breasted blue army officer's coat, the top buttons of it unbuttoned, displaying in a side pocket the top of a willow flask. A field-glass was slung from a leather strap on the outside of his rubber coat. Underneath this coat, but outside of his uniform, his sword was buckled." Most of these items were later taken by Union troops as souvenirs. *Courtesy of the Kentucky Historical Society.*

Curious Union soldiers inspect Zollicoffer's corpse. After he was killed, Zollicoffer's body remained in the road for some time. It was eventually moved under a white oak tree that became known as "The Zollie Tree." *Courtesy of the Kentucky Historical Society.*

all had a fair view of what was once Zollicoffer. I saw the lifeless body as it lay in a fence corner by the side of the road, but Zollicoffer himself is now in hell—a fitting abode for all such arch traitors!"[132]

A description provided by Vaughan of the 4th Kentucky details how Fry could have mistaken the Southerner for a Federal officer. "He was lying flat on his back, his arms extended," Vaughan explained. "He had upon his person a white rubber overcoat, unbuttoned, a blue Federal army cap, and a double-breasted blue army officer's coat, the top buttons of it unbuttoned, displaying in a side pocket the top of a willow flask. A field-glass was slung from a leather strap on the outside of his rubber coat. Underneath this coat, but outside of his uniform, his sword was buckled." With a blue uniform and hat, it is not surprising that Fry assumed that Zollicoffer was a Union officer.[133]

While Zollicoffer's body became a curiosity, his clothes, buttons, belongings and even hair became souvenirs. One correspondent believed that Zollicoffer had met a just fate. He hoped that other Confederate officers would soon find themselves "sent straightway to hell and their lifeless bodies lie in a fence corner, their faces spattered with mud, and their garments divided up, and even the hair on their head cut off and pulled out by an unsympathizing soldiery of a conquering army." Like Dr. Richardson, who took Zollicoffer's gum coat, Private Thomas C. Potter of Battery B of the 1st Ohio Light Artillery remarked, "i [*sic*] was within rods of Zollicoffer when he fell and cut three buttons off from his coat." He sent two of the buttons home. Union soldier M. G. Reis took his own memento when he "tore off a piece of the undershirt from so near the [bullet] hole that there was blood on it." Vaughan snatched Zollicoffer's sword, which he later gave to Fry, and placed Zollicoffer's cap "over his eyes." The looting of the general's body, including his hair and beard being plucked out, led Thomas to post a guard over Zollicoffer's corpse. The picking continued, however, after the battle.[134]

When the fighting resumed, Chaplain Honnell of the 1st Kentucky Cavalry pulled Zollicoffer out of "the road to prevent its being trampled over by the surging mass of combatants." Other soldiers helped Honnell, and they dropped the corpse near the fence line on the east side of the road. The remains were placed under a white oak tree. In later years, this tree gained special significance.[135]

Shortly after Zollicoffer was killed, Croxton told Fry that the regiment's right flank was in trouble. The 19th Tennessee was pressing toward that side of the road, so Fry sent two companies from the left to the right, which shored up his position near the Mill Springs Road. The death of Zollicoffer, who had been with the 19th Tennessee, disheartened that regiment, and they fell back. As Confederate cavalryman R. R. Hancock explained, "The fall of our gallant leader was a desperate blow to the followers." The Rebels fighting in the ravine on the Confederate right flank were unaware of Zollicoffer's demise, however, and they continued to assail the Federal line.[136]

Chapter 8

After Zollicoffer was killed and the 19th Tennessee fell back on the west side of the Mill Springs Road, Confederate colonel David Cummings took control of that sector of the battlefield. Cummings ordered Colonel Sidney Stanton's 25th Tennessee to continue the assault against the Union right flank. Yet again, the Rebel regiments were deployed piecemeal, preventing the Confederates from overwhelming the Union line. Across the road, the 15th Mississippi and the 20th Tennessee pressed up to the fence along the farm road and engaged the 4th Kentucky. As one Union soldier proclaimed, "The combatants were so near to each other at one time that the powder burned their faces in the discharge of their pieces; but the underbrush was so thick that bayonets were of but little use, and a charge could hardly have been made." A member of the 10th Indiana recalled that "we were so close to the enemy that we bayoneted them through the fence. The Mississippians were armed with great knives which they intended using on us, but our bayonets out-reached their knives."[137]

Although the Confederates had more men on the field, their numerical superiority was negated by their ineffective firearms and the overall lack of command. After Zollicoffer was killed, Crittenden placed Cummings in charge of Zollicoffer's brigade and told Carroll to advance his regiments against the Union position. Carroll's brigade did not take part in the fighting until after Zollicoffer had been killed. The brigade had been waiting in reserve behind a hill several hundred yards south of the Union position. Although Crittenden was seemingly absent on the field until Zollicoffer was slain, one soldier who defended the Confederate commander wrote, "Crittenden was constantly under heavy fire; and from an exposed position directed throughout, with perfect coolness, the details of the battle." With Carroll's brigade remaining inactive for so long, however, Crittenden's absence was conspicuous.[138]

Carroll deployed his regiments in a line of battle on the hill southeast of the cabin. He placed the 28th Tennessee on the right flank on the east side of the road and the 17th Tennessee on the left, deployed on the west side of the lane. Like Zollicoffer, Carroll put his two lead regiments on either side of the road. This allowed the troops to follow a landmark into the action, which was beneficial when the smoke and fog obscured the enemy lines. The 29th Tennessee was posted behind the 28th Tennessee, and the 16th Alabama was "100 paces" behind them, in reserve. Confederate cavalry remained behind the infantry, and McClung's artillery battery deployed in the rear-center of the Rebel line. Urging his troops forward, Carroll could "only judge the probable force and position of the enemy by the flash and report of their guns." Like Zollicoffer, Carroll advanced without an adequate understanding of the terrain and the enemy position.[139]

On the Rebel left, the 17th Tennessee moved to a fence approximately ninety yards from the Union line. There, it fired into the Federals, "spreading terror through the ranks of the enemy." With smoothbore muskets at that range, however, it is unlikely that many of its buck and ball rounds found their mark. At one point, the regiment was raked by Federal fire. "We were in an open space, with nothing to shelter us except an occasional stump or fallen tree," one Tennessean wrote. The men lay down to avoid the gunfire, but casualties mounted. Robert Biggers was shot in the shoulder, and F. H. Martin was struck "in the right ear, the bullet passing out the back of his head." Martin called out, "O sing to me of heaven[,] when I am called to die!" According to one soldier, when the men were prone, a rabbit ran down a lieutenant's back, ducking under his raised overcoat collar. Another soldier grabbed the hare and told the officer to quit yelling because "it is only a rabbit, and not a cannon-ball."[140]

Carroll related that the Union troops fought "with unusual vigor and courage." He added that "the ground was soon covered with the dead and wounded, and the discharge of small-arms and the roar of cannon were incessant." Although Carroll stated that the gunfire was continuous, he also remarked that the weather prevented his muskets from firing. The brigade commander claimed that one-half of his flintlocks did not fire and that some troops simply walked away from the field, leaving their useless weapons behind.[141]

Despite Zollicoffer's death, some of his regiments remained in the action. While the 15th Mississippi and the 20th Tennessee assailed the Union left and were likely unaware of their commander's demise, Stanton's 25th Tennessee made headway against the Federal right. Attacking across the west side of the road, Stanton was severely wounded in the arm. His troops, however, closed in on the right flank of the 4th Kentucky and momentarily seized Zollicoffer's body. The lack of visibility doomed the regiment. Crittenden reported that the 25th Tennessee quit firing because they believed that they were shooting at friendly units. Several Yankee volleys disabused them of that notion, and they were shoved from the field.[142]

While watching the flashes of gunfire erupt through the haze, Carroll saw that the heaviest fighting was "in front and east of my right wing," where the Federals defended the fence line along the farm road from attacks out of the ravine. Carroll knew that the mist heightened battlefield confusion. "The morning was exceedingly cloudy...rendered still darker by the dense volumes of smoke arising from the firing in front, so that the eye could distinguish objects clearly only at a short distance," he reported. With the 17th Tennessee advancing on his left, Carroll ordered the 28th Tennessee forward to support the 15th Mississippi. The troops shouted and moved out to strike the Kentuckians, but the attack ground down near the fence line.[143]

Just as Crittenden was absent from the field, one rumor claimed that Thomas was delayed because it took him a long time to fit into a new uniform. Whatever the reason, once Thomas arrived, he took charge of the troops. Moving southward down the Mill Springs Road, Thomas met the majority of the 10th Indiana, who were awaiting ammunition. According to Thomas, he found the Hoosiers "drawn up in line of battle in front of their tents." Kise told Thomas that his men had only five to ten rounds of ammunition each. Thomas ordered them forward to fight "with what ammunition they had." The commander then reached the line where the 4th Kentucky and 1st Kentucky Cavalry battled multiple regiments. When he arrived, the 20th Tennessee was trying to outflank the 1st Kentucky in the cornfield on the left while the 4th Kentucky was "maintaining its position in a most determined manner." Thomas immediately recognized the need for reinforcements. Therefore, he sent an aide to call up additional artillery, Carter's brigade and McCook's two regiments, the 2nd Minnesota and the 9th Ohio. This meant that Thomas was deploying all of his soldiers except for a 375-man battalion of Michigan Engineers and Company A of the 38th

Ohio, who were left near the crossroads to guard the Federal camps. Unlike Crittenden, Thomas was massing his men for a savage blow.[144]

With both flanks pressed by Rebel troops, Thomas sent his reinforcements in everywhere. First, to support his left flank, he called up Carter's brigade. Consisting of Batteries B and C of the 1st Ohio Light Artillery, the 12th Kentucky Infantry and the 1st and 2nd Tennessee (Union) infantry regiments, this brigade was sent east of the Union line to drive back the Confederate right wing. To support the Union right flank, Thomas sent in his best-drilled and most seasoned regiment, the 9th Ohio. Finally, to shore up his center, Thomas deployed the 2nd Minnesota to replace the exhausted 4th Kentucky, 1st Kentucky and the few companies of the 10th Indiana along the fence. In massing his men against both flanks to drive the Confederates back, Thomas wisely placed the 9th Ohio—his best regiment—on one side of the line and placed the larger number of inexperienced reinforcements on the other flank.[145]

McCook initially waited with his two regiments near the crossroads. When he learned that the Confederates were advancing, he wrote, "I ordered my brigade forward." McCook left one company from each regiment to guard their camps and then marched down the Mill Springs Road with the 9th Ohio on the right and the 2nd Minnesota on the left. As they neared the battlefield, Thomas told Manson to call up Standart's battery. Although, Manson wrote, Standart did this "with great difficulty," he deployed behind the Union line and let loose "a heavy fire." While Standart deployed, Kenny's battery, fighting to the left rear of the 4th Kentucky, was pressed by the 20th Tennessee and fell back.[146]

When the 9th Ohio and 2nd Minnesota reached the field, the Ohioans took position behind a fence on the west side of the road, thereby extending the Union right flank. The 2nd Minnesota moved to the farm road and deployed behind the fence. Thomas wrote that when the regiments arrived, "the enemy opened a most determined and galling fire, which was returned by our troops in the same spirit."[147]

The six hundred members of the 2nd Minnesota were in good hands. Their colonel, Horatio Van Cleve, was born in Princeton, New Jersey, in 1809. He was an 1831 West Point graduate and a veteran of the regular army. Living in Minnesota when the Civil War erupted, Van Cleve was named commander of the 2nd Minnesota. Upon reaching the battlefield, his regiment first supported Standart's battery, which was, Van Cleve reported, "returning the fire of the enemy's guns, whose balls and shell were falling near us." Another member of the unit recalled that "we marched about one

Union Colonel Robert McCook, who led a brigade at Mill Springs, helped organize the 9th Ohio Infantry Regiment. Wounded at Mill Springs, McCook did not survive the Civil War. *Courtesy of the Library of Congress.*

and a half miles, through deep mud and rain, to stand support to a battery that was in a field throwing shells at the enemy." The troops were unused to battle. "I never will forget the first shell that passed high above us, and our poor regiment settled nearly a foot in the muddy ground," a Minnesotan wrote. Shortly thereafter, the troops saw the 9th Ohio pushing up on their right, so the 2nd Minnesota also moved forward. Rushing down the road, they met portions of the 10th Indiana, who were out of ammunition and falling back. One officer wrote that the Hoosiers were "scattered through the woods waiting for ammunition." The 2nd Minnesota then moved to the fence along the farm road.[148]

When the Minnesotans reached the fence, the 15th Mississippi was charging out of the ravine, and the 4th Kentucky was falling back. The Confederates were at the rails when the 2nd Minnesota arrived. "Our boys rose with a yell and charged them," Lieutenant James Binford of the 15th Mississippi wrote. "Going in front of the company I was leading at the time, I soon got to the fence and there from ten to twenty yards was the enemy line [the 4th Kentucky] falling back...Our entire line, putting their guns through the cracks of the fence fired into them with ball and buckshot, and the scene that followed defied description. The screams and groans, officers cursing and begging, trying to rally their men...Lt. Freeman of company [*sic*] B jumped up on the fence and called for company B to follow, but just that time another fresh regiment arrived." The 2nd Minnesota reached the scene in the nick of time.[149]

The intensity of the fight was evident. One Minnesotan recalled that "the trees were flecked with bullets and the underbrush was cut away as with a scythe, the dead and wounded lay along the fence, on one side the blue, on the other the gray; further on the enemy's dead were everywhere scattered across the open field [in front of the fence] and lay in a [line] along the ridge [on the east rim of the ravine] where the second line had stood." Upon reaching the fence, the soldiers also saw Zollicoffer's corpse. "The body had been dragged out of the way of passing artillery and wagons, and lay by the fence, the face upturned toward the sky and bespattered with mud from the feet of passing men and horses," one wrote. The Minnesotans also recognized that regimental cohesion had broken down among the 4th Kentucky and the 10th Indiana. Low on ammunition after fighting for several hours, these troops were spread out throughout the area and were near the breaking point. Lieutenant Colonel James George of the 2nd Minnesota testified that these two units were "scattered all along through the woods up to the fence." The arrival of McCook's brigade stabilized the Federal line. When the 2nd Minnesota reached the fence, Van Cleve noted, his right flank crossed the Mill Springs Road.[150]

Just as some members of the 10th Indiana remained on the field when the 4th Kentucky arrived, some Kentuckians stayed in the fight when McCook's brigade reinforced them. Lieutenant Samuel Jennison of the 2nd Minnesota noted that most of the 4th Kentucky "passed through our files just before we reached the fence." Since it was, Lieutenant Colonel George remarked, "misty and foggy and smoky and difficult to see," the Minnesotans probably did not notice the approximately 120 Kentuckians who were "to the rear and forming at an angle of about 40 degrees with the 9th Ohio." While Fry remarked that the 2nd Minnesota arrived "in the midst of my regiment," most of the 4th Kentucky was falling back when the Minnesotans reached the line.[151]

Although the 2nd Minnesota strengthened the Federal position, they approached the fence at the same time as the 15th Mississippi. Arriving "under severe fire," one Minnesotan recalled that "the air was loaded with mist and smoke, and the underbrush in our part of the field was so thick that a man was hardly visible a musket's length away." The troops immediately took fire. "File-firing instantly became the order of the day," a Minnesotan wrote. "The men picked out the nearest cover—log, tree, fence, rail, or whatever—and would load kneeling; then step out to a clear view to fire, every time getting near and nearer to the fence, and with every round, getting less and less careful of going under cover to load." With his troops firing "as cool as boys shooting at squirrels," Van Cleve's regiment reached the "fence along the road, beyond which was an open field broken by ravines." The 2nd Minnesota immediately went into action. According to George Strong of Company D, "we were just in the edge of the woods, close to a fence, the other side of which were the rebel forces resting their guns on the fence. My position was...only fifteen to twenty feet from the foe. We all dropped on our knees and behind rotten logs, loading and firing as rapidly as possible, pouring in a fearful fire, which told upon them." McCook noted that "a hot and deadly fire was opened. On the right wing of the Minnesota regiment the contest at first was almost hand to hand; the enemy and the 2nd Minnesota were poking their guns through the same fence." Van Cleve reported that "the enemy, opening upon us a galling fire, fought desperately, and a hand-to-hand fight ensued which lasted about thirty minutes."[152]

Visibility was poor, and both sides shot and stabbed each other through the rails. William Bircher of the 2nd Minnesota wrote, "Our regiment charged up to a rail fence, and here occurred a hand-to-hand conflict: the rebels putting their guns through the fence from one side and our boys from the other. The smoke hung so close to the ground on account of the rain that it was impossible to see each other at times." S. P. Jennison remarked that "the smoke did not lift at all, but after two discharges hid the combatants almost from each other." Enemy troops tried to grab the guns of opposing soldiers, and Van Cleve recalled, "We were so close to them that one of the men had his beard and whiskers singed by the fire of one of the muskets; another caught hold of one of their muskets and jerked it through the fence; Two [*sic*] stood and fired at each other, their muskets crossing, both fell dead." Behind the Mississippians, the 20th Tennessee advanced and was met by musketry as some of the Minnesotans overshot the 15th Mississippi. Minnesotan Albert Parker wrote that his brother "died charging bravely on the enemy, from a bayonet wound in the left groin, which passed through his kidneys." Even some of the youngest soldiers took part in the fight. In the 2nd Minnesota, Company H's drummer boy picked up a musket and fought in the line.[153]

Tarrant remarked that the musketry and artillery was "like the terrible roar of the winds of a mighty storm." After more than thirty minutes, the exhausted Confederates fell back into the ravine, leaving the fence—and at least one battle flag—in the Minnesotans' possession. From the ravine, the Confederates, including the 16th Alabama, exchanged gunfire with the 2nd Minnesota for more than half an hour, keeping up what McCook called "a desperate fire."[154]

Bailie Peyton Sr. was a Tennessee Unionist and a U.S. congressman. His son, Bailie Peyton Jr., was killed at Mill Springs while fighting for the Confederacy. The father's sword, which the son wore during the battle, was captured by Union troops but was returned to the family after the Civil War. *Courtesy of the Library of Congress.*

The withdrawal of the 20th Tennessee brought martyrdom to the son of one prominent Tennessean. Bailie Peyton Jr., called a "knightly young officer," was a lieutenant in Company A. Peyton's father was a Tennessee Unionist and a U.S. congressman. When the 20th Tennessee fell back, Peyton remained on the field and may have continued walking toward the Union line. Some Federal troops thought he was surrendering. When the Minnesotans called on Peyton to give up, he raised his pistol and fired, striking Lieutenant Tenbroeck Strout "through the body." Immediately, the Federals shot Peyton through the left eye, killing him. According to Minnesotan W. S. Welles, after Peyton shot Strout, an officer told Adam Wicket of Company I to cut Peyton down. "Wicket fired and Peyton breathed his last," Welles wrote. "The whole charge, a bullet and three buckshot, entered the left side of his face, taking out the eye, and coming out just below the left ear." A lieutenant captured Peyton's sword, which citizens of New Orleans had presented to Peyton's father during the Mexican War. The blade was inscribed, "Presented to Col. Bailie Peyton, Fifth Regiment Louisiana's Volunteer National Guards, by his friends of New Orleans. His country required his services. His deeds will add glory to her arms." In trying to add glory to the Confederacy, this Tennessee Unionist's son was killed on a Kentucky hillside.[155]

Chapter 9

Of the Union regiments that fought at Mill Springs, the best-trained unit was unquestionably the 9th Ohio Infantry. Numbering 630 soldiers, including eight bugles, it was composed of German immigrants who had settled in Cincinnati. Many of these men had seen service in Europe, and they continued to drill as civilians in America. During the Civil War, the 9th Ohio was the first Buckeye regiment to enlist for three years. Initially comprising 1,035 soldiers and a band of 24 musicians, the unit's commands were given in German. Union General George McClellan remarked that it was the best regiment that he had "seen in either Europe or America," while the *Lafayette Courier* of Indiana called the unit "one of the best regiments in the service. It is composed in fact of German veterans, all of whom have seen hard service in Europe."[156]

The regiment's first commander was Colonel Robert L. McCook. Born on December 28, 1827, in New Lisbon, Ohio, Robert was the fourth son of Daniel and Martha McCook. Robert quit school at age fifteen, worked a few years and, by 1858, was practicing law in Cincinnati. Realizing that civil war was brewing, McCook studied military tactics. When the conflict started, McCook, who was familiar with Cincinnati's immigrant population, "proposed an all-German regiment." Upon its formation, McCook was elected colonel. Although McCook spoke only English, the language barrier did not hinder the regiment's success. The men fought well in western Virginia at Rich Mountain and Carnifex Ferry. Sent to Kentucky, they joined Thomas at Lebanon. McCook was promoted to brigade command, and at Mill Springs, the regiment was commanded by Major Gustave Kammerling.[157]

Leaving Company G to guard the camp, the 9th Ohio deployed Company K to watch its far right flank. Therefore, the unit advanced in line with eight companies. Later, after Company K became lost, those troops fought with the 2nd Minnesota for part of the battle.[158]

One correspondent recorded that the Germans marched with the best order of any regiment, advancing "as if upon holiday parade." A proud McCook, who was with the Germans, reported that although they "had not tasted food all day, they conducted themselves throughout like veterans, obeying each command and executing every movement as though they were upon parade." When they reached the field, they deployed west of the road and to the right of the 2nd Minnesota, where part of the 10th Indiana had been fighting. Their left flank rested near the Mill Springs Road. Lieutenant George Harries of the 9th Ohio noted that the regiment gave "loud hurrahs" and blunted a Rebel advance that tried to outflank the Minnesotans. The Confederates fell back to the edge of some woods, sixty yards away. Two fenced cornfields were between the Rebels and the Germans. The Confederates were "stationed behind straw stacks and piles of fence rails," and, McCook reported, the Rebels also took shelter among "a small log house, stable, and corn-crib."[159]

Upon their arrival, the 9th Ohio was met with a "brisk and heavy fire" of buck and ball rounds. McCook and his aide-de-camp were wounded. "I was shot through the right leg below the knee," he reported. "Three other balls passed through my horse, and another through my overcoat." The mounted Yankee officers made an inviting target. According to one doctor, McCook did not initially realize he was injured, despite the fact that the musket ball took off part of his leg below the knee. The doctor added, "A braver man I never saw."[160]

The Confederates, McCook believed, were strongly posted around the outbuildings. The 9th Ohio faced the 17th and 19th Tennessee, while the 25th and 29th Tennessee assaulted the 2nd Minnesota. Frustrated with the Rebels' position around the cabin, barn and corncrib, McCook decided that a bold move was needed to break the Confederate line. Companies A, B, C and D of the 9th Ohio would be sent on a flanking move around the Rebels' left to push them away from the structures. McCook would then order the entire regiment to advance.[161]

Before McCook's regiments deployed, the 10th Indiana returned to the fight. The Hoosiers had previously fallen back to their camp, where they realigned their companies into the proper order. Thomas, who did not know that the regiment had already fought for an hour, ordered them back into the fray. The Hoosiers returned to the intersection of the Mill Springs Road and the farm road. There, Captain I. W. Perkins stated, "we halted on the left and about fifty feet in rear of the 4th Kentucky Regiment," where they engaged the Confederates who were advancing on the position. When Thomas arrived on the field, he found the 20th Tennessee pressuring the Kentuckians' left. Therefore, as the 2nd Minnesota and the 9th Ohio arrived, Thomas ordered the 10th Indiana to the left side of the 4th Kentucky. When Kise moved his unit there, part of his left flank remained on the right side of the 4th Kentucky. "I moved the regiment through the brush and over logs to the place designated, and, coming to a fence parallel with my line, we hotly engaged the enemy, and after a hard struggle of half an hour's duration drove him before us and put him to flight with great loss," Kise reported. Some of the Hoosiers had no ammunition, so Perkins was relieved when they fought on the Kentuckians' left only for "a short time."[162]

After the Hoosiers repulsed the 20th Tennessee, the 15th Mississippi assailed the Kentuckians' right flank. To counter this threat, Thomas moved the Indianans back to the right, which returned the regiment to where they had fought during the first hour of battle. The move also reunited Kise's separated companies. Several soldiers testified that this move placed their left side where their right flank had been earlier in the day, which likely means that the 10th Indiana fought on the west side of the Mill Springs Road. Perkins said that with this deployment, they were placed more than 150 yards from the right flank of the 4th Kentucky. There, Kise wrote, the Hoosiers "soon got into a fierce contest with the enemy in front."[163]

Testimony from Kise's court-martial states that the Hoosiers also fought after the 4th Kentucky withdrew and McCook's regiments arrived on the field. Lieutenant Lewis Johnston of the 10th Indiana testified that they moved to the right side of the line and "a few minutes afterwards" the 4th Kentucky "was gone." Shortly thereafter, Johnston added, he heard "sharp firing" near their left flank. While he was "pretty certain it was the 4th Kentucky," it was likely the 2nd Minnesota, which had arrived at the fence and immediately engaged the Mississippians. Because of the poor visibility, the distance between the regiments and the farm road sloping away from the Union right, the Hoosiers probably could not see which troops were fighting on their left. Moreover, since the Indianans were engaged with the enemy when McCook's regiments arrived, they probably did not see the 2nd Minnesota take the Kentuckians' place at the fence. One soldier noted that "we could see" the 4th Kentucky and that "it was foggy and smoky but we could tell that the regiment was there." Once the lines became intermingled, however, the Hoosiers did not know that the Minnesotans had replaced the 4th Kentucky. Therefore, after McCook's brigade arrived on the field, Thomas's front consisted of the 2nd Minnesota on the left, a depleted 10th Indiana in the center and the 9th Ohio on the right. Carter's brigade, ordered to the extreme left, moved to the eastern side of the Federal line. Most important for the Hoosiers, once they moved to their new position, their quartermaster arrived and resupplied the men with ammunition.[164]

After Thomas sent in the 10th Indiana, he ordered Colonel Samuel P. Carter's brigade, consisting of the 12th Kentucky, 1st Tennessee and 2nd Tennessee Infantry regiments, to the extreme left of the Union line. He did this to prevent the 20th Tennessee from overlapping that flank. Carter's brigade had initially been kept in reserve, guarding the road between the Union camps and Somerset. Early in the action, Carter's brigade was almost broken up. When Manson returned from Thomas's headquarters, Manson found the 1st Tennessee and ordered them forward. Carter, however, ordered them back to his brigade, saving the regiment from Manson's piecemeal deployments.[165]

The brigade, numbering approximately 1,500 men, marched toward the Confederate right, cutting across fields and ravines with the 12th Kentucky on their left. Colonel William Hoskins, commander of the 12th Kentucky, wrote that despite the fog, his men did not surprise the enemy. He reported that the 12th Kentucky "imprudently huzzaed, from which the enemy got our position, and opened fire upon us with their artillery." Union cannons responded. Wetmore's battery, deployed on Carter's right, fired toward the ravine. This battery, numbering approximately one hundred men, was well drilled and competently commanded. One artilleryman wrote, "Our Captain was but 19 years of age and weighed only 90 pounds. He was lame in one hip and was not strong bodily, but he was thoroughly drilled in light artillery, and the boys had full confidence in him. He was the bravest of the brave." Carter's brigade pitched into the Rebels near the ravine, outflanking the 15th Mississippi and the 20th Tennessee, striking their right and rear and pushing them back. Tarrant noted that as Carter's men advanced, the 2nd Minnesota "kept up a most heavy fire in front."[166]

The Southerners retreated toward the Mill Springs Road and halted on a series of ridges south and southeast of the ravine. To continue the chase, Carter's men crossed rough terrain, including the hollow at the blacksmith's shop. Carter reported that he ordered his troops across a hollow to hit the

The Battle of Mill Springs ended after the Union line charged the weary Confederates. *Courtesy of the Kentucky Historical Society.*

Confederates, but the gully was steep and slippery. His officers dismounted to avoid falling. Because of the terrain, the 12th Kentucky, on the left, "lost sight of the First Tennessee." Joined by part of the 1st Kentucky Cavalry, Carter's brigade pressed forward. Here, Unionist Tennessean met secessionist Tennessean, and the 1st Tennessee captured "some prisoners." With the Rebels falling back, Carter reported that his troops moved toward the Mill Springs Road, where they saw McCook's brigade engaging the Confederates. The 12th Kentucky pressed toward the road, and the Southerners let loose a volley before retreating.[167]

On the Union right flank, McCook, his leg bleeding from the recent wound, surveyed the scene through the smoke. The fight was nearly at a standstill as the Confederates exchanged gunfire from the barn and corncrib. McCook determined that the Rebels must be crushed with brute force, and he knew that he had the men for the job: the disciplined Germans of the 9th Ohio. A bayonet charge, McCook concluded, would "turn [the Confederates'] left flank" and drive them from the field.[168]

McCook told the 9th Ohio "to empty their guns and fix bayonets." Major Kammerling told them, "If it gets too hot for you, shut your eyes, my

The orderly bayonet charge of the 9th Ohio Infantry Regiment, a unit composed of German immigrants, helped break the Confederate line at Mill Springs. *Courtesy of the Kentucky Historical Society.*

A Union charge broke the Confederate line and ended the Battle of Mill Springs. *Courtesy of the Kentucky Historical Society.*

boys—forward!" McCook then yelled, "Charge, my bully Dutchmen!" and the buglers called out the charge. The regiment shouted, and the four right companies moved around the Rebels' left flank to push the Southerners from the buildings. The Buckeyes' line surged toward the Rebels.[169]

To the left of the 9th Ohio, the 2nd Minnesota and the 10th Indiana "kept up a most galling fire in front" while the Germans charged. On the extreme Union left, Carter's brigade pushed the Confederates out of the ravine. The 9th Ohio met the Rebels at the fence that separated the two fields, and a hand-to-hand fight erupted. One witness remarked that "only a fence separated [the] contending troops. Each side often pushed rifles through it and into faces opposite—and fired—and thrust bayonets and stabbed with bowie knives at one another." Another soldier wrote that the Germans broke the Rebel line while charging "with loud shouts. The enemy immediately fled precipitately, leaving their dead and wounded, and their knapsacks, blankets, provisions." An elated McCook reported that this advance "broke the enemy's flank, and the whole line gave way in great confusion, and the whole turned into a perfect rout."[170]

The Union troops were euphoric. A member of the 2nd Minnesota believed that "the Dutchmen are rough-looking fellows on a charge," while a newspaper claimed that it was "the grandest and most effective charge of the day...For a moment there was a fierce hand-to-hand encounter, then the enemy fled." Tarrant recalled that the Ohioans "with a wild shout, and one volley, started their whole army into a stampede." According to Henry Boynton of the 35th Ohio, "It was the bayonet charge of the 9th Ohio which turned the fortunes of that day, and contributed largely to making that battle the Confederate Bull Run of the West."[171]

The charge broke the left flank of the Confederate line and, Tarrant wrote, "drove them from the field in the utmost disorder and confusion." Crittenden was elsewhere when the Ohioans advanced, so Carroll tried to mount a defense. Both flanks collapsed toward the Mill Springs Road, and Carroll moved the 19th Tennessee to the left to stabilize the line. The Rebel position continued to crumble, so Carroll deployed the 17th Tennessee and the 25th Tennessee. This was to no avail. The exhausted Confederates, still having trouble firing their flintlocks, retreated southward. Although the 17th Tennessee momentarily checked the Union advance, the Federals shoved the Confederates back.[172]

Thomas reported that the Ohioans, "with bayonets fixed, turned their flank, and drove them from the field, the whole line giving way and retreating in the utmost disorder and confusion." McCook noted that the Rebels were "seemingly prepared to resist" the charge, "but before the regiment reached him the lines commenced to give way." The 9th Ohio pushed the Confederate left flank past the cabin where the pickets of the 10th Indiana had been posted. They then drove them southward several hundred more yards to a Confederate hospital site. Seeing cavalry operating on their flanks, the Ohioans stopped and prepared for a charge by forming a hollow square. The Rebel troopers, however, did not attack.[173]

According to Lieutenant Lewis Johnston of the 10th Indiana, immediately before the 9th Ohio charged, Kise ordered his regiment to cease-fire because they were unsure of who was at their front. Seeing a flag through the smoke, they waited. Soon, however, "a blast of wind" blew away the smoke. Standing before the Hoosiers was a group of Rebel soldiers, "only twenty or thirty yards from them. We killed twenty-one around this flag."[174]

Shortly thereafter, the Hoosiers also fixed bayonets and advanced. It is likely that the 10th Indiana charged down the Mill Springs Road along a one-hundred-yard gap that existed between the 2nd Minnesota and the 9th Ohio. With one member of the unit testifying that seven companies were on the left side of the road, and with Lieutenant McAdams of Company C reported to have been killed in the middle of the road, evidence dictates that the regiment pressed down the lane behind and to the left of the 9th Ohio. Miller of the 10th Indiana said that the 9th Ohio actually charged through the 10th Indiana, leaving seven Hoosier companies in the road and three companies, A, D and F, fighting directly to the right of the 9th Ohio. Another Indianan contended that "all moved forward[;] some at charge bayonets and some kept shooting." Therefore, unlike the Ohioans' advance, the charge of the 10th Indiana was disorganized. With the Confederates falling back, Kise's regiment moved southward before stopping in an open field where they found the Southerners posted on a hill behind a fence. The Union troops pushed the Rebels back to another fence. There, some Hoosiers claimed, they joined part of the 9th Ohio and fought the Confederates "for some time." At one point, the Hoosiers and Rebels were only fifteen yards apart. Kise wrote that this was "a terrific struggle" for nearly thirty minutes and that "I never in all my military career saw a harder fight."[175]

The charge included some grisly fighting. Corporal Solomon Stafford of the 10th Indiana saw a Confederate prowling behind a tree. Stafford knocked the man down with the butt of his musket and then, seeing that the Rebel was still alive, impaled the enemy soldier. Stafford later testified, "I stuck my bayonet in him, he cried 'for God's sake don't kill me.' I said, 'God damn you, it is too late to talk now.' He would have killed me if I

A final Union charge drove the Confederates southward. Several Rebel troops were bayoneted by the advancing Federals, as pictured here. *Courtesy of the Kentucky Historical Society.*

Union Colonel William Kise of the 10th Indiana remarked that after his regiment joined the charge to drive the Rebels from the field, when they reached a fence "many of the enemy were found lingering in the corners, and were bayoneted by my men between the rails." This patriotic cover (envelope) depicts one such incident. *Courtesy of the Kentucky Historical Society.*

had not killed him." Kise noted that when they reached a fence, "many of the enemy were found lingering in the corners, and were bayoneted by my men between the rails."[176]

The 29th Tennessee, commanded by Colonel Samuel Powell, had spent most of the battle in reserve near the hospital site south of the cabin. When both Confederate flanks fell apart, the regiment moved forward where, Major Horace Rice wrote, they took a position on "the brow of a hill, at the edge of the woods, about one hundred yards to the right [eastern side] of the road." There, they stopped in a wheat field near the cabin and waited. When the 9th Ohio barreled through the fields near the cabin, Carroll ordered Powell's regiment to strike. Rice noted that "the enemy crossed the road and advanced to within thirty paces of our line when he was checked by a raking fire from our boys and held in that position until portions of Col. Battles and the Mississippi Regts passed out to our right." The 29th Tennessee fired, "checking [the Union troops] with a raking fire at 30 paces." They halted the Union advance long enough to allow the 15th Mississippi and the 20th Tennessee to escape. Powell, however, was "badly wounded" in the action. According to the *Memphis Daily Appeal*, "Powell was not aware of being wounded until some time after, when, on attempting to draw his pistol, he found his arm hanging powerless at his side." His left arm was "shattered... near the shoulder." Crittenden also threw in the 16th Alabama, but the Federal tide could not be stopped. The 17th Tennessee, 28th Tennessee and the Alabama troops retreated. The 29th Tennessee waited as other regiments withdrew, only falling back when they were nearly surrounded. According to Rice, the regiment was "under fire" for only ten minutes.[177]

While fighting near the cabin, Kise reported that the Southerners held "a piece of high ground" and that "they received considerable re-enforcements and made a last and desperate effort to repulse our troops." When the Rebels withdrew, the Hoosiers captured nearly twenty prisoners. Indianan Derrick Harrison wrote, "I had the pleasure of capturing 5 of these queer birds alive. They were caring for a wounded man when I surprised them and told them that they were my prisoners." Kise's men then joined the 9th Ohio to chase the Rebels to the hospital site, where they helped drive off the Confederate cavalry. While waiting for ammunition, companies A, D and F, which had charged with the Buckeyes, rejoined the 10th Indiana. The Confederate infantry retreated southward down the Mill Springs Road. Their cavalry halted four hundred yards south of the hospital "in line of battle in an old field." Union artillery advanced, deployed on a ridge near the hospital and drove off the horsemen.[178]

After the battle, several officers claimed that the 10th Indiana did not participate in the final charge. These accusations led to Kise and Manson being court-martialed for falsifying their after-action reports. It is likely, however, that the terrain, smoke, confusion of battle and intermingling of Union troops prevented soldiers from recognizing other regiments. Again, officers also wanted their units to get credit for the victory. During Kise's court-martial, for example, McCook testified that "there was no other troops engaged when the 9th Ohio made its charge except the 2nd Minnesota and [stragglers] from the other Regiments." In addition to discounting the 10th Indiana, McCook also ignored the role of Carter's brigade. Van Cleve of the 2nd Minnesota downplayed the Hoosiers' role by stating that, although the Indianans started the battle, they were not fighting as a cohesive unit by the time McCook's soldiers appeared. Certainly, their numbers had dwindled from casualties and stragglers. It is likely, however, that the 10th Indiana was fighting to the right of the 4th Kentucky when the 2nd Minnesota entered the fight. Van Cleve probably never saw Kise's regiment deploy in that area. Therefore, Van Cleve assumed that the 9th Ohio, which had marched to the battlefield on the Minnesotans' right, was always immediately next to his regiment. Kise determined that Fry, McCook and other officers probably did not see the 10th Indiana because they were more than one hundred yards to the right of the 4th Kentucky (and later the 2nd Minnesota). Kise testified, "Because from the distance they were from this...position, the nature of the ground and the woods around that vicinity; it was impossible for them to" see. Hoosiers' letters and diaries corroborate Kise's report that the 10th Indiana did indeed participate in the charge. Although their advance was made with fewer men and was more disorganized than the disciplined 9th Ohio, they charged nonetheless. The Indianans fought down the Mill Springs Road, in the fields on the east side of that road, and helped push the Rebels back to the hill immediately south of the cabin. Then, they joined the 9th Ohio to drive the Confederates past the field hospital, where a lack of ammunition and sheer exhaustion halted their advance.[179]

Chapter 10

The 9th Ohio, 10th Indiana, 2nd Minnesota and Colonel Samuel P. Carter's Kentucky and Tennessee troops pushed the Confederates southward. Although the bayonet charge of the 9th Ohio was the most dramatic advance and gained the most attention, all of these units helped break the Confederate line.[180]

According to several Union officers, including General Thomas and Lieutenant Colonel James George, the 2nd Minnesota and the 9th Ohio were in the action for only thirty minutes before the Confederate troops fled. By the time McCook's regiments arrived, the Rebels were exhausted and frustrated over their useless flintlocks. Therefore, when the advance began, the Rebels could not withstand the Union onslaught. Brents called McCook's charge "as gallant a charge as was ever witnessed. The enemy could not stand it, but broke and fled in great confusion."[181]

The Union soldiers paused near the hospital, refilled their cartridge boxes and waited for Standart's artillery to drive off the Confederate cavalry. Once the horsemen departed, the Federals pursued Crittenden's army down the Mill Springs Road. McCook noted that the Rebels retreated "in utter confusion," while Fry commented that "the enemy gave way, flying before our forces like chaff before the wind." Hoosier Thomas J. Stephenson simply told his grandfather that it was "a vary hard fite [*sic*]" and that the Confederates "begun to run like turkeys." Crittenden recognized the chaos, reporting that some "regiments became confused and broken and great disorder prevailed." The Southern commander blamed this on "a want of proper drill and discipline" brought about by too much active service and not enough training.[182]

When the Confederate lines broke, W.J. Worsham of the 19th Tennessee carried his wounded comrade Charley Clemenson to the hospital site. "Poor Charley was dying when we laid him down," Worsham wrote. "We can never forget the sad anxious expression of his face as we left him...dying alone, deserted by all whom he thought were friends, left on the cold ground with naught but the cold rain to wash the sweat of death from his brow."[183]

The Confederates streamed back to Beech Grove. The battle had lasted approximately four hours, from 6:30 a.m. to nearly 11:00 a.m. When the fight ended, additional Federal reinforcements arrived. The 14th Ohio and the 10th Kentucky, which had been sent to find the Confederate forage train, never found the wagons. Instead, when they heard of the conflict, they rushed to the battlefield, arriving when the fight ended. Harlan wrote, "It was a magnificent sight to see how the boys struggled through mud and rain to reach the field of battle. The ground was so wet and muddy under them that their feet slipped at every step." More of Schoepf's soldiers also arrived from Somerset, having stretched ropes across Fishing Creek to cross.[184]

The Federals marched toward Beech Grove "in line of battle," one Union soldier remarked, which was "safe but slow." Another commented that the Rebels fled "in the wildest confusion, like a flock of sheep." Accoutrements and weapons scattered along the road detailed the rout. Artilleryman Thomas C. Potter remarked that "the ground was literally covered all the way to their camp with...muskets, sabres, blankets, knapsacks, haversacks, canteens, cartridges, horses and everything that they could throw away to facilitate their escape." Green Clay concurred, writing that "they fled panic stricken for 8 [miles] to their entrenchments—leaving knapsacks—guns—wagons & 2 pieces of artillery on the road." Major Henry G. Davidson of the 10th Kentucky simply noted that "language fails me to describe their total rout. They threw away everything—guns, knapsacks, haversacks, and even their coats." According to R. M. Kelly, the haversacks were "filled with rations of corn pone and bacon." Colonel William B. Wood of the 16th Alabama likened the retreat to "a grand funeral procession."[185]

By the time the Union troops reached Beech Grove, they were, Kise wrote, "powder-besmeared, tired, and hungry." The Federals stared at the earthworks, replete with well-defended artillery positions and abatis. Harlan noted that the entrenchments "appeared to be quite formidable." The bluecoats had expected the Confederates to make a stand at Moulden's Hill, a ridge three-quarters of a mile north of the entrenchments, but the

Union Colonel John Marshall Harlan commanded the 10th Kentucky (Union) Infantry Regiment. Harlan, who later became a justice of the U.S. Supreme Court, requested that his regiment lead the attack on the Beech Grove entrenchments after the Battle of Mill Springs. The Rebel works, however, were abandoned. *Courtesy of the Library of Congress.*

position was abandoned. Carter called the hill an "important height, which commanded [the] fortified camp," so Wetmore and Standart's batteries deployed there and shelled the Confederate works. Thomas, who also placed Kenny's battery on a ridge "at Russell's house," hoped to soften the Rebel entrenchments with artillery fire. In the morning, he would storm the camp with his fresh troops, the recently arrived 10th Kentucky, 14th Ohio and Schoepf's 17th, 31st and 38th Ohio infantry regiments. While the Federal batteries blasted the camp with sixteen cannons, only a handful of Rebel guns responded. The Union artillery fire ceased at dark, and the Federal troops went into camp, expecting to assault the fortifications the next day.[186]

While Thomas's troops bivouacked, the Confederates were desperately active. Crittenden assessed the situation, noting his army's low morale, incomplete fortifications, the presence of Union artillery on high ground and scant provisions. After discussing the situation with his officers, Crittenden ordered his men to cross the Cumberland River. The Southern commander did not think that his battered and exhausted men could adequately defend Beech Grove. After the war, Crittenden explained, "The few shot and shells that fell in the camp so plainly demonstrated the demoralization of the men, that I doubted, even if I had rations, which I had not, whether the camp could have been successfully defended for twenty-four hours." That afternoon, the *Noble Ellis* and "two flat boats" began crossing the men over the river. The vessels' size limited what could be transported, so most of the baggage, supplies, horses and mules were left behind. Within six hours, the Rebel army had crossed to Mill Springs.[187]

Upon seeing the boats, Union troops were unsure if the move was a Confederate withdrawal or the arrival of reinforcements. Fry told his wife that "we saw their little steam boat crossing back and forth all night but did not know whether they were falling back or bringing new regiments to this side." Within the Rebel works, however, it was chaos. "We are on the river bank in one compact mass of excited and confused humanity," a member of the 19th Tennessee wrote. "Thousands were crowded there waiting, each his turn to get on the Noble Ellis [*sic*] as she crossed and recrossed the river...What a racket and confusion reigned here, and right in the face of the enemy."[188]

Confederate morale was further damaged when Union cannons bombarded the boats, striking the *Noble Ellis*. According to the *New York Times*, one shot went through the vessel's chimney while another "exploded over the wheel." Private Joseph Durfee of Wetmore's battery wrote, "We saw a steamer just crossing the river. We fired at her with the Parrott guns, and after firing ten shots, set her on fire...When we shelled her, she was loaded with horses and baggage. The horses jumped overboard, some were saved and some drowned." Unionist accounts note that the artillery ignited one boat and sunk another, while the Confederates claimed that they burned the ships after they had crossed. Captain C. C. Spiller, a cavalry officer who had taken command of the *Noble Ellis*, reputedly torched the vessel to keep it out of Union hands.[189]

Overcrowding and the Federal artillery made for a dangerous crossing. To avoid the danger, "a large number" of Confederates tried to swim the river and drowned. One reporter commented that "this is attested by other persons seeing their bodies below Mill Spring in the river." Another correspondent claimed that "all of these found a watery grave...the many bodies found washed on islands and both banks of the river, during the last few days, indicate that they were not few." Harrison also noted these casualties, writing that "we could see their boat crossing the river and it was 2 miles distance and it only took 5 shots to fire their boat and we could see them swimming the river and many of them found a watery grave."[190]

When dawn broke on January 20, the Union troops prepared to assault the Confederate works. Having missed the battle, Harlan and Colonel James Steedman of the 14th Ohio asked if their regiments could lead the attack. Union artillery fired a few shells into the camp, and when Rebel cannons did not respond, the Federal infantry advanced. Clamoring over the earthworks, the Northerners found the camp deserted. For Harlan, it was a missed opportunity. "It turned out that if Thomas had, before dark, attacked the rebels in their fortifications, he could have carried the day and perhaps captured all the fleeing rebels with their guns," he wrote. John Dow of the 31st Ohio was relieved, however, writing that the Confederates "were very sternly fortified and we could never whiped [*sic*] them if [they] had not got scarred [*sic*] and left."[191]

Some Federals marveled at the extensive earthworks. Others toured the cabins that the Confederates had built for winter quarters, some of which contained glass windowpanes. One member of the 10th Indiana was unimpressed, noting that "this is certainly one of the filthiest camps I ever beheld." The Federals, however, realized that the Rebels had rushed off. Manson reported that "the panic among them was so great that they even left a number of their sick and wounded in a dying state upon the river bank." Upon realizing that the Rebels' morale had been broken, Fry asked Thomas why he had not asked the Confederates to surrender during the previous night. "Hang it, Fry," Thomas responded, "I never once thought of it."[192]

The greatest indicator of the Confederates' rapid retreat was the massive quantity of supplies left at the camp, valued at $2 million. The Rebels left ten cannons, caissons with ammunition, one hundred wagons, more than 1,200 horses and mules, hundreds of muskets, three days' worth of rations, hospital supplies, chickens, cooking pots, dishes, tools, sugar, coffee, bedding, swords and private baggage. Several of the horses were given to Union officers, Zollicoffer's papers were captured and, John Dow wrote, the Federals recaptured some cannons that had been lost at the Battle of

Bull Run. Wetmore's battery claimed two of the pieces for its own use. There were also multiple flags captured, including one that belonged to the "Mississippi Butchers." A second had been presented "to the Mounted Rangers," while a third, left at Beech Grove by the "Wigfall Rifles," was later put on display in a collection in New York, with ticket sales benefitting the U.S. Sanitary Commission. The victors presented Buell with one of the flags, while others were given to the Indiana state government, including the flag of the Marion City [Alabama] Guards and the Tennessee Marsh Blues. In addition, Charles Scheffer, the Minnesota state treasurer, was on hand to pay the 2nd Minnesota. Scheffer managed to take several "trophies" back to the Minnesota capitol, including flags, military papers and, reputedly, Bailie Peyton's sword. Perhaps the most cherished plunder was a barrel of apple brandy, which the Germans of the 9th Ohio swarmed upon, filling their canteens. While Hoosier Wesley Elmore commented that the Rebels "left Every thing they Had," the usable animals and supplies were sent to Lebanon, while other items were destroyed.[193]

Some Federal troops plundered the camp for personal gain or for souvenirs. One Indiana soldier took a gold watch and a silver one. He sent the gold one home to his father and kept the silver watch. Another soldier was not so lucky. According to Dow of the 31st Ohio, "Jim Hughes found a gold watch but Gen Thomas took it from him. He managed to get an old sword which he kept—I got a splendid double Blanket." Dow, a bugler, also scored tobacco and a cornet.[194]

One Confederate left the Federals a note. "We fought you bravely, and desperately but misguidedly," it read. "We leave here under pressing circumstances, but do not feel that we are whipped." Across the river, Captain Francis Aldridge of the 15th Mississippi lamented that he had lost a miniature of his wife and those of his children, which had been left in his personal baggage. Within a day, the plunder was flowing into Somerset. One Union soldier there wrote that "citizens and soldiers are straggling in, loaded with trophies of the battle."[195]

Just as Zollicoffer's body had been an object of curiosity on the battlefield, the slain general's belongings found at Beech Grove were also of interest. Some newspapers reported that Kise found Zollicoffer's "breast-plate," which was "made of common sheet iron, of four thicknesses riveted together, is about eighteen inches in length, and fourteen inches broad." Kise wondered if Zollicoffer had forgotten to wear it. Another newspaper commented that the Hoosier colonel gave the piece to the State Library in Indianapolis while another said he sent it to Indiana governor Oliver Morton.[196]

For some of the men, the plunder was heartbreaking. Directed to read Rebel correspondence, a Union soldier perused a letter written by one of Zollicoffer's daughters. She told the general about her new baby and how they hoped for his speedy return. The soldier gave the letter to his adjutant, telling him that he "had no heart for it" and that the adjutant should find someone else to read the letters. He added, "I felt more like weeping than rejoicing."[197]

With baggage, weapons and supplies littering both sides of the river, Manson was ordered across the Cumberland to retrieve abandoned property while McCook's brigade went to Somerset. On January 20, Thomas issued a congratulatory order from the "Camp Opposite Mill Springs." Therefore, the Mill Springs name took precedence in the press, which conferred that name on the battle and enshrined it to historical memory. Although the earthworks and cabins were ultimately destroyed, some of Thomas's regiments fixed up the site and camped there to watch for the Rebels.[198]

The Federals did not have to worry about the Confederates' return. Upon crossing the Cumberland, Crittenden's army broke apart. Thomas reported that the Southerners "retreated with great haste and in all directions," while Green Clay said that the "army was scattered to the winds and will not be again organized." He added that they were "completely dispersed."[199]

The Confederates' situation was desperate. Not only had they lost the battle, but they also had little food for the retreat to Tennessee. "The country is entirely destitute of provisions," Crittenden wrote. Carroll, who concurred, reported that the barren region made the troops "more apprehensive of destruction by famine than at the hands of the enemy." This "fear of starvation," Carroll added, caused mass desertions. Although many of the men slipped away into East Tennessee, the army procured some cattle, hogs, bacon, flour and potatoes. This food, however, did not prevent some deserters from stealing horses or mules before riding away.[200]

With the defeat came controversy. Multiple reports noted that Crittenden was drunk both during the battle and on the retreat. One reporter heard that he was intoxicated during the fight "and was barely able to ride off so as to make his escape." Sober or not, by January 26, Crittenden's broken army reached Gainesboro, Tennessee, approximately seventy-five miles east of Nashville.[201]

Fortunately for the Confederates, Thomas did not follow. Buell wrote that Thomas had difficulty crossing the river so he could not give chase. In addition, bad roads, poor weather and the difficulty in transporting supplies hampered Federal hopes of a pursuit. Buell also considered a chase to be pointless because Crittenden's army had melted away. In his assessment, there was no organized foe to face.[202]

Crittenden's retreating army carried the news of Zollicoffer's death. While secessionists mourned his demise, the general's corpse remained a source of wonderment for the Union soldiers. Immediately after the battle, a group of Minnesotans stood gawking at the body when an officer rode up and yelled, "What in h—l are you doing here? Why are you not at the stretchers bringing in the wounded?" A soldier replied, "This is Zollicoffer." The officer spat, "I know that, he is dead, and could not have been sent to h—l by a better man, for Col. Fry shot him—leave him and go to your work."[203]

Just as Beech Grove was plundered after the battle, so, too, was Zollicoffer's body. I. B. Webster of the 10th Kentucky saw the corpse and wrote that "his head was near a tree, with his body and limbs extending from it. His clothing had been nearly all clipped off by momento-lovers." When members of the 35th Ohio neared the field, they passed stragglers who reported Zollicoffer's death. When they told one soldier that the general could still be alive, he said that the general was "dead, and in h—l." He then held up a lock of hair and added, "There is a bunch of the son-of-a-guns [*sic*] hair, I cut them off his head myself."[204]

Tarrant remarked that "some of the privates, out of mere thoughtlessness, not thinking how bad it looked, tore his clothes in order to procure souvenirs of the noted general." Eventually, Union officers placed a guard over the body, but, Tarrant confirmed, there was at least one spot on Zollicoffer's head where "a lock had been plucked out." Even Tarrant's chaplain claimed a battlefield token. The day after the fight, he took a white oak stick from the tree where Zollicoffer had been shot that "had five bullet marks and clots of blood upon it." While not a relic of the true cross, it provided the clergyman with a remembrance of the Battle of Mill Springs.[205]

Even Fry, anointed as Zollicoffer's killer, picked up a few souvenirs. After the battle, the colonel had Zollicoffer's coat, watch and field glass. The *Cincinnati Daily Press* claimed that "Zollicoffer's entire uniform was taken off his body in small pieces for trophies." Harlan even sent some artifacts home, including a fur robe found in Zollicoffer's tent and Crittenden's campstool. Hoosier Derrick Harrison wrote to his fiancée and included a souvenir. "Here is a small bit of Zolicofers [*sic*] coat," Harrison wrote. "He fell, yes the traitor is dead and God knows we do not resent it for he has committed all kinds of crimes." Another Union soldier claimed, "I have a small piece of Zollicoffer's undershirt," while Ernst Kegel of the 9th Ohio had "accouterments and an overcoat belonging to the rebel General." By

February 1862, a Union major in Louisville had Zollicoffer's "buckskin shirt" that the Tennessean had been wearing when shot. "It was very soft," a newspaper noted, "and must have been exceedingly comfortable if kept dry."[206]

After the war, Fry published letters claiming that Zollicoffer's body was not plundered. In 1870, he said that Zollicoffer's corpse had been well treated and that the body had been washed and his clothes changed. Fry remarked that the clothes were "all furnished from my wardrobe." Despite numerous claims to the contrary, Fry said that Zollicoffer's garments were not taken as souvenirs, but instead, "when his body was taken from the field it was cold and stiff, and his clothing was so covered with mud and saturated with blood that it was necessary to cut his garments from him." While Fry said that he dressed Zollicoffer in his (Fry's) own clothes, another Union soldier said that Zollicoffer's washed corpse was dressed in garb found in Battle's trunk at Beech Grove. Others claimed that Zollicoffer's uniform was divided up only after it was removed from his body. Soldiers' accounts, however, diverge from this story, but it is likely that pieces were cut from the uniform during the battle, after the fight and once the remnants of his uniform were removed.[207]

Although the corpse was plundered, Union troops did care for the remains after the fight. Harlan saw the body "on a plank on the ground." Later, another witness saw it in the camp of the 2nd Minnesota. A large crowd of soldiers stood around as two washed the mud from the shirtless corpse. Witnesses could plainly see three wounds. James Cooper of the 20th Tennessee, who had been injured and captured, saw the body after it had been moved onto "a cot in a small tent." While the general's remains were cared for, Cooper scoffed, "the other Confederate dead were treated with scant ceremony, being brought up on stretchers and tossed into large pits twelve or fifteen feet square and a foot or two of dirt heaped over them."[208]

Thinking that Confederate authorities would claim Zollicoffer's body, the Federals kept the corpse in the Union camp for several days. When no Rebels appeared, Zollicoffer and Bailie Peyton, the congressman's son, were sent to Somerset to be embalmed. Finally, on January 27, Confederates appeared under a flag of truce to claim Zollicoffer's body. By that time, the corpse was on its way to Nashville, escorted by Confederate surgeon Daniel B. Cliffe. Manson told Crittenden "that his body has been properly cared for, decently clothed, and placed in a substantial wooden box." Zollicoffer's and Peyton's corpses went to Nashville via Lebanon. There, Zollicoffer's body was placed

The Union army cared for Zollicoffer's remains after the Battle of Mill Springs. His body was embalmed in Somerset and was then transported to Nashville, where the general was buried. *Courtesy of the Kentucky Historical Society.*

in a "metallic case." One member of the 64th Ohio noted that Cliffe carried a stick that was stained with Zollicoffer's blood.[209]

The bodies were taken through Bacon Creek and Munfordville, two stops on the Louisville and Nashville Railroad in Hart County. Upon reaching Munfordville on January 31, the escorts stopped at Union General Alexander McCook's headquarters. McCook, the brother of Colonel Robert McCook, wrote to Bailie Peyton Sr., informing him that his son's remains were on their way to Nashville. "I had no personal acquaintance with you," McCook wrote, "but I have often heard my father speak of you as one of his friends; and I, as the son of a friend, have had all possible attention paid to his remains." McCook told Peyton that his son's body was again "embalmed by Professor Goldsmith, of Louisville, and Dr. Meylot, my medical director." Buell had provided a "metallic coffin," McCook noted, and he wanted the grieving Unionist to know that his son's remains were not ignored on the battlefield. "The body of your son was buried with one hundred and fourteen others;" McCook wrote, "and you should be under lasting obligations to surgeon Dan'l B. Cliffe, Confederate army (now prisoner of war), for having your son disinterred and forwarded to this point."[210]

Union officers, including Captain Daniel McCook (another one of Robert's brothers), escorted the remains to Rebel lines. They met Confederate General Thomas Hindman under a flag of truce south of Cave City. The Southerners sent the bodies to Nashville, where they arrived on February 1. Zollicoffer lay in state in the capitol and was then buried in Nashville's Old City Cemetery.[211]

While Zollicoffer had a large funeral, most casualties were not so fortunate. When the fight ended, scores of bodies lay scattered across the field. One correspondent wrote that "dead rebels...were lying thick in the underbrush in every direction." John Dow of the 31st Ohio wrote that "it was a horrible sight to see the men leying [*sic*] around with a musket-Ball shot through their heads." Another Buckeye wrote that "the bodies of many of the dead were still lying on the field, and had swollen, in many instances, to enormous proportions; some had turned black."[212]

One civilian found that the battlefield was:

> *horrid and revolting in the extreme. A large number of the dead were shot in the head. One was shot directly in the eye and the brain was oozing from the wound. Five dead and one wounded lay behind one log, all but the wounded one were shot in the head. One rebel had a ball through his neck which destroyed the power of speech...A dark complexioned man with a heavy black beard, who said he was from Mississippi, was lying on the ground with a broken thigh. He was stern and sullen—he had only one favor to ask—that was that some one of us would kill him. I said to him, we will soon take you to the surgeon, and do all we can to relieve you...A young man, quite a boy, begged me to let the Lincolnites kill him.*[213]

The day after the battle, the Michigan Engineers and Mechanics began burying the dead. The Union troops were initially interred near their camps. In 1868, however, the remains were moved to a hill that eventually became the Mill Springs National Cemetery. The Confederate casualties were buried in mass graves near where they had fallen. A soldier in the 35th Ohio wrote that the Michigan "pioneers" buried the Confederates in a garden "near a log shanty." The Union troops placed the bodies in a six-foot-wide, two-foot-deep trench. If a dead Confederate had a blanket on him, he was wrapped in it before he was interred. The Buckeye wrote, "The bodies were laid as closely to each other as the rigidness of the dead would admit. There they lay, faces turned upward, hands placed upon the breast—a ghastly looking sight: over these soil was thrown, and the graves filled. This kind of work was going on all over the field." More than one hundred Confederates were buried in a mass grave about seventy-five feet from where Zollicoffer was killed. Today, a tablet placed over their remains reads that they "died far from their homes," but "glory keeps ceaseless watch about their tomb."[214]

While the dead were buried, the survivors faced harrowing scenes in makeshift field hospitals. According to one Union soldier, "the few scattered shanties, and other buildings found on the field where the battle was fought, were taken for hospitals where the wounded were gathered in, until ambulances could bear them to more suitable places. Surgeons had tents, near these places, where the fierce work of amputating limbs was going on."[215]

Difficulties were compounded because the battle was fought in a rural area with few amenities. One member of the United States Sanitary Commission remarked that the wounded "were in a region of country not easy of access, and where the comforts of life did not abound." Therefore, many of the injured were moved to Somerset, but this proved to be difficult because Thomas's army had few ambulances. Union Dr. David P. Smith reported that moving them was dangerous because "the dreadful roads over which all of the wounded had been brought had induced profuse suppuration." Haphazardly conveyed in all types of vehicles, a member of the 9th Ohio reported that "the suffering soldiers had to be carried on litters or transported in wagons, without springs," and were jostled along "a miserable rugged road" to Somerset. The troops' "cries were heart-rending when the bandages became loosened and their ball shattered limbs escaped from their ligatures and hung loose and dangling." Once they reached Somerset, however, they were "comfortably lodged in the court-house, churches, and private houses." Dr. Smith "found the little village crowded with sick and wounded." In addition to Somerset, an estimated 175 ill and injured Confederates were left at Monticello. One witness wrote that the town "is at present nothing but a hospital for the Confederate sick and wounded." He added that "on the road to Monticello we saw wounded in every house...Most of these houses contained from two to five" injured. He also remarked that Rebels were also found "in every hut-house, hovel and stable, between Mill Spring and the Tennessee State line, [where] the sick, wounded, and dying are passed." By January 26, ninety-six wounded Confederates were also in Knoxville hospitals.[216]

Soldiers in Somerset died from wounds, complications from operations, disease and illnesses. Cooper of the 20th Tennessee remarked that "many of my comrades and acquaintances died from their wounds and sickness combined." One soldier who had his leg amputated "died of diarrhoea [*sic*] about a month after the operation." Dr. Smith noted that another man "with a buckshot in his brain," survived for about two weeks, but died after a series of "convulsions." Smith added that another passed away "from the irritation [infection] produced by fragments of the upper jaw."[217]

Those who died in Somerset, Monticello, Mill Springs or on the road to Tennessee added to the grim tally. Buell noted that "the enemy left 200 killed and wounded on the field," while his chief of staff remarked that the Rebels' "loss in killed and wounded was great." The Federals had approximately 4,000 men on the field while the Rebels had 5,500. While several sources report that the Union army lost 39 killed and 207 wounded and the Confederates suffered 125 killed, 308 wounded and 95 missing, Ron Nicholas, former administrator of the Mill Springs Battlefield Association, estimates that casualties were higher. Nicholas contends that the Union army had 53 dead, while the Confederates lost 148 killed.[218]

Reported casualties show that the 10th Indiana bore the brunt of the Confederate assault. Suffering the highest number of Union casualties, it was reported that the Hoosiers lost 11 killed and 75 wounded. The four companies of the 1st Kentucky Cavalry lost 3 killed and 19 wounded; the 4th Kentucky lost 8 killed and 52 wounded; the 2nd Minnesota suffered 12 killed and 33 wounded; and the 9th Ohio reported 6 killed and 28 wounded. Wolford estimated that at least half of his wounded "will die."[219]

The attacking Confederates suffered even more, prompting one to note that the battle was a "terrible slaughter." Of these losses, Zollicoffer's brigade, which was in the action the longest, suffered the most. Fighting unsupported and with the regiments deployed in a piecemeal fashion, reports indicate that Zollicoffer lost at least 98 killed, 265 wounded and 66 missing, a total of 429 men. Conversely, Carroll's brigade, which was not deployed until later, had 28 killed, 46 wounded and 29 missing, a total of 103 casualties. Zollicoffer's Mississippians and the 20th Tennessee clearly fought the longest, with each of those two regiments losing more than Carroll's entire brigade. Three-fourths of the Rebel losses were from the 15th Mississippi and the 20th Tennessee. The 20th Tennessee, for example, suffered 33 killed, 59 wounded and 18 missing. Furthermore, of the 125 Confederates killed, 44 of them were from the 15th Mississippi. In addition, 153 of the 309 wounded were from that regiment, and 29 of the 99 missing were also Mississippians. With the 15th Mississippi losing 220 out of 400 men, they suffered 55 percent casualties, while the 20th Tennessee had 39 percent casualties.[220]

Other Rebel regiments also suffered. The 29th Tennessee had 5 killed, 12 wounded and 10 missing in ten minutes of fighting. Major Horace Rice believed that some of the wounded and missing "crawled to the river several miles above [Beech Grove] and made their way out, but they have never been heard of." Also, Rice noted, Colonel Powell "was severely wounded and has been taken home."[221]

The 19th Tennessee, which fought against the more lightly defended Union right flank, lost 10 killed, 22 wounded and 2 missing. The 25th Tennessee, whose commander, Sidney Stanton, was seriously wounded, suffered 10 killed, 28 injured and 17 missing. The 17th Tennessee lost 11 killed, 25 wounded and 2 missing, and the 28th Tennessee lost 3 killed, 4 wounded and 5 missing. The 16th Alabama, which fought late in the battle, suffered 9 killed, 5 missing and 12 wounded. The Rebel cavalry lost only a handful of men.[222]

Several issues caused the discrepancy in Confederate casualties versus Union losses. First, the Southerners attacked Union defenders who, in many instances, were behind cover. Moreover, the Rebels' poor muskets led to fewer Union casualties. The Federals' rifles were more accurate, and because many of the Confederates' flintlocks would not fire, the Federal troops simply threw more lead at the attacking Rebels, causing greater casualties. Some of the missing may have been Rebel troops who drowned while crossing the Cumberland River after the battle, increasing the overall number of Confederate casualties.

Although the Union army killed and wounded more Confederates and drove the Rebels back to Tennessee, the Federals did not follow up on the victory. Because of the weather, poor roads and the difficulty in transporting supplies, Thomas neither chased Crittenden nor moved into East Tennessee. Buell held firm on taking Bowling Green before capturing

Nashville. Therefore, Thomas moved to Munfordville to prepare for the advance on Bowling Green. He was, however, rewarded for his victory at Mill Springs. On February 3, the U.S. Senate confirmed his nomination to brigadier general.[223]

The Mill Springs campaign was over. Zollicoffer was dead, Crittenden disgraced and Thomas's adherence to the Union—despite his Virginia birth—confirmed.

Chapter 11

Three days after the battle, President Lincoln and Secretary of War Edwin Stanton issued a "congratulatory order" that called Mill Springs a "brilliant victory." Union soldiers added to the chorus. Green Clay posited that "such a complete rout never was known to *any army*." John Dow added that the fight was "a great victory on our side," and Major Henry Davidson of the 10th Kentucky called it "the first blow which breaks the back of this rebellion." Unionist newspapers agreed. The *Vermont Phoenix* was hopeful that Federal troops would soon take East Tennessee, while the *New York Times* called it "the most complete rout the rebels have yet experienced." The *Cincinnati Daily Press*, still holding out hope for a short war, optimistically wrote that "it may be that the recent brilliant success near Somerset is the real beginning of the end." The *Chicago Tribune* even reported that the battle affected opinions across the ocean, writing that the Union victory gave some British politicians early ammunition for supporting the Federal cause.[224]

Just as Unionists were jubilant, Rebel soldiers and civilians were crestfallen. While some blamed the loss on the army's lack of training and poor weaponry, others pointed to Crittenden. Confederate congressmen called for Crittenden's head, and Tennessee governor Isham Harris told authorities that "Crittenden can never rally troops [in] East Tennessee. Some other general must be sent there." Crittenden, however, tried to sidestep blame. After the war, he wrote that "the battle of Fishing Creek was a necessity, and that I ought not to be held responsible for that necessity." Instead, he blamed the loss "in a great degree, to the inferiority of our arms and the untimely fall

U.S. Senator John J. Crittenden was appalled when his son, George, joined the Confederacy. Although he disagreed with George's choice, Senator Crittenden defended his son when George was attacked in Unionist newspapers after the battle. *Courtesy of the Library of Congress.*

of General Zollicoffer." On a tactical level, Zollicoffer's death did not impact the battle. Although he was beloved by his troops, several of his regiments, including the 15th Mississippi and the 20th Tennessee, did not see him fall. Furthermore, since Zollicoffer was not exercising brigade-level leadership at the time of his death, and since he was deploying his regiments piecemeal, he did not have a grasp on his command, which makes Crittenden's argument ring hollow. Instead, Secretary of War Judah Benjamin wrote, Crittenden's superiors heard "painful rumors" about "the intemperance of General Crittenden." It was said that the Kentuckian was intoxicated during the battle. The *Charleston Mercury* lambasted Jefferson Davis for "selecting a known drunkard for a Major General." The *New York Times* even reported that during the retreat Crittenden was inebriated at a hotel in Monticello. Because of his father's prominence and his brother's rank as a Union general, Crittenden was also accused of being a covert Unionist. Others reported that the Confederate commander had been bribed with $47,000 to lose the battle. The sordid tales were widely reported, prompting Crittenden's father to lash out at the editor of the *Louisville Journal*. "My son is a rebel!—I defend him not!" the senator wrote. "But what public good can be done by such denunciations as that article contains? Its exaggerations and misstatements make it unjust and ungenerous, and as to his family, it is most cruel." An official court of inquiry was eventually opened, Crittenden and Carroll were later arrested for drunkenness while at another post and Crittenden's military career never recovered.[225]

The Federal victory broke the right flank of the Confederate defensive line that crossed southern Kentucky. It also led to a series of Union advances. With the Rebel army pushed from eastern Kentucky, the Confederate position at Bowling Green grew vulnerable. With the line cracked, Southern armies withdrew to Tennessee. The Union army pushed over the first domino at Mill Springs; shortly thereafter, other Confederate positions fell. In February, Fort Henry and Fort Donelson surrendered. Nashville dropped to Union forces, and by the end of March 1862, Johnston's army had fallen back to Corinth, Mississippi. In an attempt to reverse their sagging fortunes, in early April, Johnston's Confederates attacked Grant at the Battle of Shiloh. Like Crittenden, Johnston hoped to strike a divided Union army before reinforcements arrived. In the two-day struggle, Johnston was slain, and more than twenty-three thousand Union and Confederate soldiers were killed and wounded. After Shiloh, few believed that the Civil War would be brief. The first cobblestone on the path to that battle was laid at Mill Springs.[226]

Several elements caused the Confederate defeat. The terrain aided the Union defense, while weather hindered visibility, rendered the Rebels' flintlocks nearly useless and caused delays as Southern regiments deployed. Furthermore, a lack of Confederate leadership and piecemeal attacks doomed the Southern assault.

Mill Springs was a battle marked by confusion. Rain, mud, smoke, hilly terrain, fog and unfamiliarity with friendly regiments and officers caused chaos and prevented units from seeing one another. Because this was an early battle and officers wanted their share of the glory, recriminations marred both sides. Manson and Kise were court-martialed but were ultimately exonerated. For the Confederates, accusations flew about Carroll's and Crittenden's supposed drunkenness, and the reputations of these men never fully recovered.

The battle showcased the inexperience of officers. Manson, for example, abrogated brigade command and ran to the rear to report the Confederate assault rather than sending a courier to headquarters. Zollicoffer failed to send an aide to reconnoiter the Mill Springs Road and accidentally wandered into Union lines only to be killed. Conversely, the fight showcased the value of the 9th Ohio's training and experience. That unit, supported by the 10th Indiana, the 2nd Minnesota and Carter's brigade, swept the Rebel line into

Confederate General Felix Zollicoffer, killed at the Battle of Mill Springs, became an early martyr for the Southern cause. His death was mourned across the South, especially in his native Tennessee. *Courtesy of the Library of Congress.*

oblivion thanks to the Ohioans' well-timed bayonet charge. Overall, army-level leadership was the key. When Thomas arrived on the field, he took control. Crittenden did not.

The fight provided the Rebel army with both a martyr and a scapegoat. Zollicoffer was one of the first generals killed in action during the Civil War, and the Tennessean became a martyr for the Rebel cause. Although his reputation dimmed as generals of greater consequence were slain, his death shook the morale of some secessionists, especially those in Tennessee. Concurrently, Crittenden's star faded as he became a scapegoat for the loss. As the drunkard son of a Unionist politician and brother of a Union general, his reputation melted away like the Rebel army he had led at Mill Springs.

For the Federals, the battle strengthened the reputation of another whose loyalty had been questioned. The Virginia-born Union commander George H. Thomas attained great fame. Extensive newspaper coverage of the fight—which proved to be the Union's first significant victory—propelled Thomas as Crittenden's tottering reputation collapsed.

The battle highlighted Confederate deficiencies in arms and equipment and showed Southern authorities that the Western Theater would be doomed if they could not replace antiquated weaponry. Equally, after the Federal debacle at Bull Run, Mill Springs provided Unionists with a needed victory and boosted flagging morale. As Union veteran Thomas Speed proclaimed, the battle "brought hope and cheer in place of dread." Importantly, it also opened East Tennessee for Union invasion.[227]

Mill Springs proved to be emblematic of the war as a whole. Fought in what was arguably the most important border state, two Kentuckians—Fry and Crittenden—were instrumental officers on either side. The battle highlighted Lincoln's concerns for Kentucky and East Tennessee, brought national attention to the plight of East Tennessee Unionists and showcased the fratricidal nature of the conflict as Tennesseans battled one another. Furthermore, as German-born Ohioans drove off the Rebels at the point of the bayonet, the battle highlighted the critical role that immigrants would play in fighting for their new homeland.

Importantly, the battle put Kentucky firmly in Union hands. Only a few months earlier, the nation had wondered if the Bluegrass State would follow the rest of the upper South and secede. The Northern victory at Mill Springs consolidated Unionist control of the state at a crucial time. Until Rebel armies invaded Kentucky in August 1862 and fought the battles of Richmond, Munfordville and Perryville, the Bluegrass State remained under Federal control and provided badly needed men and materials to the national cause. A Union-held Kentucky also created a crucial buffer between the Deep South and the Midwest.

The Battle of Mill Springs knocked the bloom off the rose. It was a small battle of great consequence. With the events that followed, Americans realized that the Civil War would be an arduous struggle. As Eastham Tarrant of the 1st Kentucky Cavalry wrote, the battle

> *was one of the most brilliant victories to the Union cause, and one of the most important in its results that happened during the war. It was its first great victory. It revived the drooping spirits of the loyalists throughout the United States, and spread consternation in the ranks of the heretofore audacious foe. It contradicted the extravagant assertions… that one valiant Southerner was equal to five Yankees on the field of battle…it was the forerunner of a series of successful movements and brilliant victories of the Union armies which not only caused the enemy to abandon Kentucky in force, but also the largest portion and most fertile region of Tennessee.*[228]

In the years after the battle, as silence reigned over the fields where scores of soldiers had been slain, efforts to memorialize the site began. First, the cemetery where the Union soldiers had been buried was officially established as a National Cemetery. In 1880, the Kentucky legislature approved the creation of the "Mill Springs National Cemetery Decoration Society of Pulaski County," which was given authority to purchase land in order to enhance Decoration Day events. To prevent riotous celebrations, the bill also banned the sale and use of "spirituous, vinous, or malt liquors, or a mixture of either within two miles of said cemetery on decoration day." By 1894, the Mill Springs National Cemetery contained 714 graves, with 366 of them being unknown soldiers.[229]

In the first few years of the twentieth century, as Kentucky continued a postwar cognitive dissonance of embracing the Lost Cause despite a primarily Unionist wartime allegiance, the focus at Mill Springs moved away from the Unionist National Cemetery to the site of Zollicoffer's demise. On one Decoration Day, a young girl named Dorotha Burton adorned the Confederate mass grave with flowers and wrapped the tree under which Zollicoffer's body had been moved—later dubbed "The Zollie Tree"—with a wreath. In 1904, Confederate veteran Bennett Young heard of Burton's efforts and traveled to the area to meet her. Young departed the meeting determined to erect a monument at the battlefield. On October 22, 1910, more than five thousand people gathered to dedicate a monument commemorating the spot where Zollicoffer had fallen. Logan's daughter donated land for the obelisk. Burton made wreaths, two of Zollicoffer's daughters attended the ceremony and, in Kentucky's Lost Cause tradition, the key monument at the site of a Union victory highlighted the death of a Confederate general.[230]

Commemorative efforts continued into the early twentieth century. On October 7, 1933, approximately three thousand people attended the dedication of Zollicoffer Park, which included the area where Zollicoffer had fallen and the Confederate mass grave. Local residents raised funds for a stone wall at the park, and a year later, Governor Ruby Lafoon helped dedicate new iron gates at the site. Although Lafoon hoped that the battlefield would become a state park, for the next several decades the area was ignored. By 1971, a writer for the *Filson Club History Quarterly* proclaimed that "the park has fallen into a state of almost total neglect." A local women's club was, however, working to clean it.[231]

In the early 1990s, Kentucky experienced a renaissance in battlefield preservation, and Mill Springs played a key role. In 1992, the Mill Springs Battlefield Association was established to preserve and interpret the battleground. The next year, the site became part of the National Register of Historic Places, with 1,529 acres included in the National Register

The Zollicoffer monument at the Mill Springs battlefield. The Confederate mass grave can be seen behind the monument. *Courtesy of the author.*

boundary. In 1994, the battlefield was designated a National Historic Landmark. Although The Zollie Tree, which Mill Springs historian Raymond Myers called "a living memorial," was knocked over in a thunderstorm in 1996, the site has continued to make improvements. By 2013, approximately 600 acres of battlefield land were preserved and a $2 million museum facility had been constructed. That year, Congressman Hal Rogers proposed a feasibility study to designate the Mill Springs battlefield as a National Park.[232]

In the early twentieth century, the experiences of two residents signified the true importance of the Mill Springs battlefield. It was neither monuments nor plaques nor new iron gates. When the county built a road nearby, the bones of two dead soldiers, long interred in forgotten graves, were found a little more than a mile away from the battleground. These men had died in a schoolhouse that, during the battle, had been converted into a hospital. Likely dying from their wounds and buried hastily, the location of their remains was quickly forgotten. Elbert

Simpson and Basil Duke Simpson collected the bones, made a coffin and buried the remains at Zollicoffer Park. Today, these once-forgotten soldiers rest with their comrades. It can be assured, however, that dozens more await discovery.

Notes

Introduction

1. Quoted in Ron Nicholas, "Mill Springs: The First Battle for Kentucky," in Kent Masterson Brown, ed., *The Civil War in Kentucky: Battle for the Bluegrass State* (Mason City, IA: Savas Publishing Co., 2000), 73.
2. Nicholas, "Mill Springs," 68, 73; "Return of Bailie Peyton's Sword," *Confederate Veteran* [hereafter cited as *CV*] 15 (May 1907): 230; "Dedication of Zollicoffer Monument," *CV* 18 (December 1910): 567.
3. Various names from Mark M. Boatner III, *The Civil War Dictionary* (New York: Vintage Books, 1988), 487; U.S. War Department, *The War of the Rebellion: A Compilation of the Official Records of the Union and Confederate Armies* (Washington, D.C.: U.S. Government Printing Office, 1880–1901), vol. 7: 98, 93, 845 [hereafter cited as *OR*. Unless noted, all references refer to Series I]; *Goodhue Volunteer* [Red Wing, MN], March 5, 1862; Jesse Hyde Diary, SC1274, Kentucky Historical Society Special Collections, Frankfort, KY; *Holmes County Republican*, January 30, 1861; *Cleveland Daily Herald*, "A Ride to the Battle," January 28, 1862.
4. *Chicago Tribune*, "What's in a Name," February 5, 1862; *Chicago Tribune*, "Gen. Thomas's Victory," January 25, 1862; *Goodhue Volunteer*, "What's in a Name," February 19, 1862; "Mill Springs and Fishing Creek," *CV* (December 1910): 550.
5. Congressional petition noted in *New York Daily Tribune*, February 11, 1862.

Chapter 1

6. James T. Killebrew, ed., Journal of Ellen Kenton McGaughey Wallace, Kentucky Historical Society Special Collections, Frankfort, KY.
7. Raymond E. Myers, *The Zollie Tree: General Felix K. Zollicoffer and the Battle of Mill Springs* (Louisville, KY: Filson Club Historical Society, 1994), 50; R. M. Kelly, "Holding Kentucky for the Union," *Battles and Leaders of the Civil War* (Secaucus, NJ: Castle Books, reprint ed.), 1: 374, 377, 378, 379; Arndt Stickles, *Simon Bolivar Buckner: Borderland Knight* (Chapel Hill: University of North Carolina Press, 1940), 87; Larry J. Daniel, *Days of Glory: The Army of the Cumberland, 1861–1865* (Baton Rouge: Louisiana State University Press, 2004), 6.
8. Steven E. Woodworth, *Jefferson Davis and His Generals: The Failure of Confederate Command in the West* (Lawrence: University Press of Kansas, 1990), 61; Myers, *The Zollie Tree*, 10, 13–15, 17, 19, 20, 21, 26, 42, 44; Marcus J. Wright, "General Felix K. Zollicoffer," *Southern Bivouac* 2 (July 1884): 485, 486, 487, 488, 489, 494; Thomas Lawrence Connelly, *Army of the Heartland: The Army of Tennessee, 1861–1862* (Baton Rouge: Louisiana State University Press, 1967), 86; Thomas A. Head, C*ampaigns and Battles of the Sixteenth Regiment, Tennessee Volunteers in the War Between the States* (Nashville, TN: Cumberland Presbyterian Publishing House, 1885), 294, 296, 297, 298, 306, 299; "Dedication of Zollicoffer Monument," *CV*, 568; Noel C. Fisher, *War at Every Door: Partisan Politics and Guerrilla Violence in East Tennessee, 1860–1869* (Chapel Hill: University of North Carolina Press, 1997), 44; Margaret Boyles, "Gen. F. K. Zollicoffer," *CV* 15 (January 1907): 28; R. Gerald McMurtry, "Zollicoffer and the Battle of Mill Springs," *Filson Club History Quarterly* 29 (October 1955): 303.
9. Stephen D. Engle, *Don Carlos Buell: Most Promising of All* (Chapel Hill: University of North Carolina Press, 1999), 144; "we must not" quoted in Fisher, *War at Every Door*, 45; Head, *Campaigns and Battles*, 299, 300; Myers, *The Zollie Tree*, 44, 45, 48; Connelly, *Army of the Heartland*, 86, 87; Wright, "Zollicoffer," 489.
10. Zollicoffer quoted in Myers, *The Zollie Tree*, 51; Stanley F. Horn, *The Army of Tennessee* (Wilmington, DE: Broadfoot Publishing Co., 1987), 50.
11. Myers, *The Zollie Tree*, 177; Freeman Cleaves, *Rock of Chickamauga: The Life of General George H. Thomas* (Norman: University of Oklahoma Press, 1948), 81; Kelly, "Holding Kentucky," 1: 382; McMurtry, "Zollicoffer," 304; Lowell H. Harrison, *The Civil War in Kentucky* (Lexington: University Press of Kentucky, 1975), 24; John Fitch, *Annals of the Army of the Cumberland*

(Mechanicsburg, PA: Stackpole Books, 2003 [1864]), 60; Hambleton Tapp and James C. Klotter, eds., *The Union, the Civil War, and John W. Tuttle: A Kentucky Captain's Account* (Frankfort: Kentucky Historical Society, 1980), 53.

12. Fitch, *Annals*, 56–59; Kelly, "Holding Kentucky," 1: 382; Cleaves, *Rock of Chickamauga*, 84, 85.

13. Harrison, *Civil War in Kentucky*, 16; Charles P. Roland, *Albert Sidney Johnston: Soldier of Three Republics* (Lexington: University Press of Kentucky, 2001), 260, 262; Lowell H. Harrison, *Lincoln of Kentucky* (Lexington: University Press of Kentucky, 2000), 158; Myers, *The Zollie Tree*, 178, 117; Woodworth, *Davis and His Generals*, 52; Kelly, "Holding Kentucky," 1: 379; Stickles, *Buckner*, 92; Brian D. McKnight, *Contested Borderland: The Civil War in Appalachian Kentucky and Virginia* (Lexington: University Press of Kentucky, 2006), 37; Connelly, *Army of the Heartland*, 14; Zollicoffer's note to Magoffin quoted in Wright, "Zollicoffer," 489–90; and quoted in Basil W. Duke, *A History of Morgan's Cavalry* (West Jefferson, OH: Genesis Publishing Co., 1997 [1867]), 59; Lincoln to Morton, September 29, 1861, Abraham Lincoln Papers at the Library of Congress, http://memory.loc.gov (accessed September 21, 2009).

14. Roland, *Johnston*, 263, 265; Harrison, *Civil War in Kentucky*, 16–17; Kelly, "Holding Kentucky," 1: 379; Myers, *The Zollie Tree*, 178; Gerald J. Prokopowicz, *All for the Regiment: The Army of the Ohio, 1861–1862* (Chapel Hill: University of North Carolina Press, 2001), 14; Edward G. Longacre, *Cavalry of the Heartland: The Mounted Forces of the Army of Tennessee* (Yeardley, PA: Westholme Publishing, 2009), 50; Woodworth, *Davis and His Generals*, 53. Confederate arms shortages from Woodworth, *Davis and His Generals*, 54; Roland, *Johnston*, 227; *OR*, vol. 7: 817; Larry J. Daniel, *Soldiering in the Army of Tennessee* (Chapel Hill: University of North Carolina Press, 1991), 40.

15. Connelly, *Army of the Heartland*, 15, 87–88; McKnight, *Contested Borderland*, 37, 38; Head, *Campaigns and Battles*, 301; Myers, *The Zollie Tree*, 178; Wright, "Zollicoffer," 490; Eastham Tarrant, *The Wild Riders of the First Kentucky Cavalry* (West Jefferson, OH: Genesis Publishing Co., 1997 [1894]), 62; Daniel, *Days of Glory*, 22.

16. Benson Bobrick, *Master of War: The Life of General George H. Thomas* (New York: Simon and Schuster, 2009), 87; Myers, *The Zollie Tree*, 178, 55; Van Horne, *Army of the Cumberland*, 27.

17. Henry Moesler's Civil War Diary, http://archivesofamericanart.typepad.com/pdfs/henry-mosler-civil-war-diary-transcript-only.pdf (accessed December 28, 2012).

18. Connelly, *Army of the Heartland*, 87; Horn, *The Army of Tennessee*, 67; Tarrant, *Wild Riders*, 68, "a Hungarian" quoted, 69; Kelly, "Holding Kentucky," 1: 383; Myers, *The Zollie Tree*, 56, 178–79.
19. McKnight, *Contested Borderland*, 43, 44; Daniel, *Days of Glory*, 24; Tarrant, *Wild Riders*, 71, 72, 74; Van Horne, *Army of the Cumberland*, 32. For a history of the Battle of Camp Wildcat, see Kenneth A. Hafendorfer, *The Battle of Wild Cat Mountain* (Louisville, KY: KH Press, 2003).
20. Tarrant, *Wild Riders*, 76, 80; McKnight, *Contested Borderland*, 45; McMurtry, "Zollicoffer," 304, 305; Nicholas, "Mill Springs," 51, 52 53; Tapp and Klotter, *John W. Tuttle*, 63; Cleaves, *Rock of Chickamauga*, 90; Myers, *Zollie Tree*, 179; Fitch, *Army of the Cumberland*, 60; Prokopowicz, *All for the Regiment*, 68.
21. Kenneth P. Williams, *Grant Rises in the West: The First Year, 1861–1862* (Lincoln: University of Nebraska Press, 1997), 132; McKnight, *Contested Borderland*, 45; McMurtry, "Zollicoffer," 305; Myers, *Zollie Tree*, 59, 179, Zollicoffer quoted, 60; Harrison, *Civil War in Kentucky*, 24.
22. Kelly, "Holding Kentucky," 1: 383; Nathaniel Cheairs Hughes Jr., *Old Reliable: General William J. Hardee* (Baton Rouge: Louisiana State University Press, 1965), 85–86; "some were lying" quoted in Cleaves, *Rock of Chickamauga*, 91. For the Wildcat Stampede, see *OR*, vol. 4: 350, 444, and vol. 7: 444.
23. Van Horne, *Army of the Cumberland*, 36; Myers, *The Zollie Tree*, 179, 66; Lowell H. Harrison and James C. Klotter, *A New History of Kentucky* (Lexington: University Press of Kentucky, 1997), 196; Roland, *Johnston*, 272; Daniel, *Days of Glory*, 29; Prokopowicz, *All for the Regiment*, 17, 35; Kelly, "Holding Kentucky," 1: 385; Bobrick, *Master of War*, 93.
24. Woodworth, *Davis and His Generals*, 62; Kelly, "Holding Kentucky," 1: 385; Engle, *Buell*, 115, 105, 102, 87, 122, 124–25, McClellan quoted, 115; Daniel, *Days of Glory*, 35, 43, 44; Prokopowicz, *All for the Regiment*, 66, 62.
25. James M. Prichard, "Maj. Gen. George Bibb Crittenden," in Bruce S. Allardice and Lawrence Lee Hewitt, eds., *Kentuckians in Gray: Confederate Generals and Field Officers of the Bluegrass State* (Lexington: University Press of Kentucky, 2008), 71.
26. Prichard, "Crittenden," 69; Albert D. Kirwan, *John J. Crittenden: The Struggle for the Union* (Lexington: University Press of Kentucky, 1962), 30, 64, 98, 159.
27. Prichard, "Crittenden," 69, 70, 71; Kirwan, *John J. Crittenden*, 122, 159, 241, 446; Damon R. Eubank, *In the Shadow of the Patriarch: The John J. Crittenden Family in War and Peace* (Macon, GA: Mercer University Press, 2009), 57.

28. Prichard, "Crittenden," 71, 72; Mrs. Chapman Coleman, ed., *The Life of John J. Crittenden, With Selections from His Correspondence and Speeches* (Philadelphia: J.P. Lippincott and Co., 1873), 2: 322; Kirwan, *John J. Crittenden*, 446, 447, 448; Joseph H. Parks, *General Edmund Kirby Smith, CSA* (Baton Rouge: Louisiana State University Press, 1954), 147; Eubank, *Patriarch*, 58.

Chapter 2

29. Tarrant, *Wild Riders*, 83; *Richmond Daily Dispatch*, December 31, 1861.
30. Connelly, *Army of the Heartland*, 89; Harrison and Klotter, *New History*, 197; Harrison, *Lincoln of Kentucky*, 164; *OR*, vol. 7: 706, 679, 453, 452, 687, 715; Myers, *Zollie Tree*, Zollicoffer quoted, 61; Tapp and Klotter, *John W. Tuttle*, 68; Harrison, *Civil War in Kentucky*, 24.
31. Myers, *Zollie Tree*, 61, 180, 66; Harrison, *Civil War in Kentucky*, 24; Nicholas, "Mill Springs," 53; Van Horne, *Army of the Cumberland*, 39; Tapp and Klotter, *John W. Tuttle*, 63; Daniel, *Days of Glory*, 47; *OR*, vol. 7: 458.
32. *OR*, vol. 7: 10, 7–8; Van Horne, *Army of the Cumberland*, 39; Daniel, *Days of Glory*, 46–47.
33. *OR*, vol. 7: 734, 12; Nicholas, "Mill Springs," 54; R. R. Hancock, *Hancock's Diary, Or, A History of the Second Tennessee Confederate Cavalry* (Nashville, TN: Brandon Printing Co., 1887), 90.
34. Connelly, *Army of the Heartland*, 78; W. H. Perrin, J. H. Battle and G. C. Kniffin, *Kentucky: A History of the State*, 7th ed. (Louisville, KY: F. A. Battey and Co., 1887), 390 [hereafter cited as Perrin]; Daniel, *Days of Glory*, 48; C. David Dalton, "Zollicoffer, Crittenden, and the Mill Springs Campaign: Some Persistent Questions," *Filson Club History Quarterly* 60 (October 1986): 468; Myers, *Zollie Tree*, 69; Tarrant, *Wild Riders*, 85; McMurtry, "Zollicoffer," 306; Eubank, *Patriarch*, 61; "The War in Kentucky: How the Battle of Mill Springs was Fought and Won," *National Tribune* [hereafter cited as *NT*] (October 11, 1883): 1.
35. *OR*, vol. 7: 10; Hancock, *Hancock's Diary*, 92; W. J. Worsham, *The Old Nineteenth Tennessee Regiment, CSA* (Knoxville, TN: Paragon Printing Co., 1902), 19; Tarrant, *Wild Riders*, 85; *Richmond Daily Dispatch*, December 17, 1861.
36. *OR*, vol. 7: 8–9, 1, 486, 12, 481, 484, 487; Myers, *Zollie Tree*, 180; Hancock, *Hancock's Diary*, 91; Daniel, *Days of Glory*, 47; Williams, *Grant Rises*, 146.
37. *OR*, vol. 7: 745; Eubank, *Patriarch*, 59, 60; Prichard, "Crittenden," 71; Woodworth, *Davis and His Generals*, 66.

38. *OR*, vol. 7: 10, 753.
39. Ibid., 754, 738, 749, 750, 751, 774, 780.
40. Prichard, "Crittenden," 72; *OR*, vol. 7: 769–70; Hancock, *Hancock's Diary*, 124; Eubank, *Patriarch*, 59; James M. Prichard, "Glory Denied: The Hard Fate of George B. Crittenden," in Lawrence Lee Hewitt and Arthur W. Bergeron Jr., eds., *Confederate Generals in the Western Theater*, Vol. 2 (Knoxville: University of Tennessee Press, 2010), 7; Connelly, *Army of the Heartland*, 96.
41. *OR*, vol. 7: 105; Brian D. McKnight, *Confederate Outlaw: Champ Ferguson and the Civil War in Appalachia* (Baton Rouge: Louisiana State University Press, 2011), 56–57.
42. *OR*, vol. 7: 786, 797, 814; Nicholas, "Mill Springs," 54; Hancock, *Hancock's Diary*, 105.
43. *OR*, vol. 7: 797; D. H. Cummings to "My Dear Wife," December 28, 1861, letter, transcript in Mill Springs Battlefield Collection, Nancy, KY [hereafter cited as MSBC]; D. H. Cummings to "My Dear Annie," December 29, 1861, letter, transcript in MSBC.

Chapter 3

44. *OR*, vol. 7: 505–06, 510; Mary Clay Berry, *Voices from the Century Before: The Odyssey of a 19th Century Kentucky Family* (New York: Arcade Publishing, 1997), 275.
45. James A. Moore to "Friend James," December 19, 1861, letter, M0701, Indiana Historical Society, Indianapolis, IN [hereafter cited as IHS]; Wesley Elmore, December 4, 1861, letter, Wesley Elmore letters, SC1801, IHS.
46. Roland, *Johnston*, 281; Van Horne, *Army of the Cumberland*, 44; Daniel, *Days of Glory*, 49; Prokopowicz, *All for the Regiment*, 67; *OR*, vol. 7: 522, 78, 524; Tarrant, *Wild Riders*, 86; Betty J. Gorin, *Morgan Is Coming: Confederate Raiders in the Heartland of Kentucky* (Louisville, KY: Harmony House, 2006), 28; Boatner, *Civil War Dictionary*, 488; Myers, *Zollie Tree*, 180.
47. J. W. Bishop, "The Second Regiment," in *Minnesota in the Civil War and Indian Wars* (St. Paul, MN: Pioneer Press Co., 1890), 82; Newell L. Chester, ed., *A Drummer Boy's Diary, Comprising Four Years of Service with the Second Regiment Minnesota Veteran Volunteers, 1861 to 1865* (St. Cloud, MN: North Star Press, 1995 [1889]), 8; Engle, *Buell*, 142; Civil War Diary of Thomas M. Small, Co. I, Tenth Regiment [Indiana], January 3, 1862

entry, SC1355, Folder 1, IHS; James Birney Shaw, *History of the Tenth Regiment, Indiana Volunteer Infantry* (Lafayette, IN, 1912), 137; Derrick B. Harrison letter, IHS.

48. Dalton, "Zollicoffer," 468; Hancock, *Hancock's Diary*, 106; Roland, *Johnston*, 281.

49. D. H. Cummings to "My Dear Wife," January 6, 1861, letter, transcript in the MSBC; Nicholas, "Mill Springs," 54; Hancock, *Hancock's Diary*, 106, 108; *OR*, vol. 7: 828, 824; Worsham, *Old Nineteenth Tennessee*, 20; Myers, *Zollie Tree*, 73.

50. *OR*, vol. 7: 537, 536, 542, 545, 549; Berry, *Voices from the Century Before*, 278.

51. *OR*, vol. 7: 539; Myers, *Zollie Tree*, 180; J. A. Brents, *The Patriots and Guerrillas of East Tennessee and Kentucky* (New York: Henry Dexter, 1863), 114; Boyle to Garrett Davis, January 20, 1862, Abraham Lincoln Papers at the Library of Congress, http://memory.loc.gov (accessed September 21, 2009).

52. *OR*, vol. 7: 554; Williams, *Grant Rises*, 171.

53. Kelly, "Holding Kentucky," 1: 387; *OR*, vol. 7: 79, 83, 84; Engle, *Buell*, 143; Myers, *Zollie Tree*, 5, 86, 88, 181; Raymond E. Myers, "Who Owns Zollicoffer Park?" *Filson Club History Quarterly* 45 (April 1971): 240; Nicholas, "Mill Springs," 57; Connelly, *Heartland*, 97; Bishop, "Second Regiment," 83; Fitch, *Annals*, 61; Tarrant, *Wild Riders*, 87.

54. *OR*, vol. 7: 79, 84; Shaw, *History of the Tenth*, 138; Loren P. Beth, *John Marshall Harlan: The Last Whig Justice* (Lexington: University Press of Kentucky, 1992), 55; Van Horne, *Army of the Cumberland*, 44; Kelly, "Holding Kentucky," 1: 387; Daniel, *Days of Glory*, 51; Nicholas, "Mill Springs," 57; Tarrant, *Wild Riders*, 87; Brents, *Patriots and Guerrillas*, 115.

55. Prichard, "Glory Denied," 8; *OR*, vol. 7: 105.

56. *OR*, vol. 7: 105; Crittenden quoted in Hancock, *Hancock's Diary*, 111; Prichard, "Glory Denied," 8.

57. Prokopowicz, *All for the Regiment*, 69; Kelly "Holding Kentucky," 1: 387; Daniel, *Days of Glory*, 51–52; Van Horne, *Army of the Cumberland*, 44–45; *OR*, vol. 7: 79, 97; Nicholas "Mill Springs," 57; Myers, *Zollie Tree*, 88; Bishop quoted in Engle, *Buell*, 143; Shaw, *History of the Tenth*, 138.

58. Tarrant, *Wild Riders*, 88; *OR*, vol. 7: 90, 84; Shaw, *History of the Tenth*, 138; Civil War Diary of Thomas M. Small, IHS; James T. Thompson, ed., *The Memoranda of James L. Hickerson, I Company, 10th Indiana Volunteer Infantry: August 1861–September 1864* (Albuquerque, NM: James T. Thompson, 1993), 4.

Chapter 4

59. Head, *Campaigns and Battles*, 302; *Richmond Daily Dispatch*, January 27, 1862; Wright, "Zollicoffer," 491; Dalton, "Zollicoffer," 468; *OR*, vol. 7: 105; Harrison, *Civil War in Kentucky*, 26; Kelly, "Holding Kentucky," 1: 387; Nicholas, "Mill Springs," 58; Jefferson Davis, *The Rise and Fall of the Confederate Government* (New York: D. Appleton and Co., 1881), 2: 20; Roland, *Johnston*, 281; Prichard, "Crittenden," 72.
60. *OR*, vol. 7: 105, 106.
61. Ibid., 104.
62. Ibid., 106; Kelly, "Holding Kentucky," 1: 387; Prichard, "Crittenden," 72; Connelly, *Army of the Heartland*, 97; Prichard, "Glory Denied," 8; Worsham, *Nineteenth Tennessee*, 20; Harrison, *Civil War*, 26; Crittenden quoted in Davis, *Rise and Fall*, 2: 20; D. H. Cummings battle report transcript, MSBC; Eubank, *Patriarch*, 62; Nicholas, "Mill Springs," 58.
63. Roland, *Johnston*, 281; McMurtry, "Zollicoffer," 307; Nicholas, "Mill Springs," 58; Prichard, "Glory Denied," 8; *OR*, vol. 7: 108; Head, *Campaigns and Battles*, 307, 308; Wright, "Zollicoffer," 496.
64. Zollicoffer quoted in "Incidents of Mill Springs," *Freemont Journal* [Ohio], January 31, 1862; Harrison, *Civil War*, 26; Prichard, "Glory Denied," 8; Myers, *Zollie Tree*, 94; *OR*, vol. 7: 111; James L. Cooper, "Service with the Twentieth Tennessee Regiment," *CV* 33 (January 1925): 15; Worsham, *Nineteenth Tennessee*, 20–21.
65. *OR*, vol. 7: 111, 106, 82; Frank Moore, ed., *The Rebellion Record: A Diary of American Events* (New York: G. P. Putnam, 1862), 4: 46; Nicholas, "Mill Springs," 58; Kelly, "Holding Kentucky," 1: 392.
66. Nicholas, "Mill Springs," 58–59; *OR*, vol. 7: 106, 79, 100; Kelly, "Holding Kentucky," 1: 387; McMurtry, "Zollicoffer," 308; Brents, *Patriots and Guerrillas*, 115; Tarrant, *Wild Riders*, 89; Eastham Tarrant, "Mill Springs," *NT* (September 8, 1892): 4; Shaw, *History of the Tenth*, 138; Crittenden quoted in Hancock, *Hancock's Diary*, 124; and Davis, *Rise and Fall*, 2: 20.
67. *OR*, vol. 7: 100, 79; Daniel, *Days of Glory*, 52; Tarrant, *Wild Riders*, 89; Jack Hurst, *Men of Fire: Grant, Forrest, and the Campaign that Decided the Civil War* (New York: Basic Books, 2007), 61; *OR*, vol. 7: 106.
68. Cooper, "Service with the Twentieth Tennessee," 15; Mill Springs Battlefield Association, "Battle of Mill Springs: Gen. Zollicoffer Slain, Union Is Victorious," in *Kentucky's Civil War, 1861–1865* (Clay City, KY: Back Home in Kentucky, Inc., 2005), 58; Derrick B. Harrison letter, IHS; Binford quoted in Nicholas, "Mill Springs," 59.

69. Dunbar Rowland, *The Official and Statistical Register of the State of Mississippi, 1908* (Nashville, TN: Brandon Printing Co., 1908), 615–17; W. J. McMurray, *History of the Twentieth Tennessee Regiment Volunteer infantry, CSA* (Nashville, TN, 1904), 390.
70. Delmore O. Miller testimony in Mark D. Jaeger, ed., transcription of "Court Martial of Lt. Col. William C. Kise," National Archives Records Administration, Record Group 153, Judge Advocate Generals Records, Washington, D.C. [hereafter referred to as Kise Court-Martial]; Nicholas, "Mill Springs," 59; "beaten back" quoted in Hurst, *Men of Fire*, 62; Shaw, *History of the Tenth*, 140; *OR*, vol. 7: 100.
71. *OR*, vol. 7: 106; Nicholas, "Mill Springs," 59; Myers, *Zollie Tree*, 94; Wright, "Zollicoffer," 492; Cummings Battle Report, MSBC; Cooper, "Twentieth Tennessee," 16.
72. Worsham, *Nineteenth Tennessee*, 21; Wright, "Zollicoffer," 496.
73. Minnesota officer quoted in Prokopowicz, *All for the Regiment*, 71; Moore, *Rebellion Record*, 4: 42; *OR*, vol. 7: 90, 84; Delmore Miller testimony, Kise Court-Martial; Nicholas, "Mill Springs," 59.
74. *OR*, vol. 7, 100, 79, 84; W. B. Carroll testimony, Kise Court-Martial; Delmore O. Miller testimony, Kise Court Martial; Lewis Johnston testimony, Kise Court-Martial; Prokopowicz, *All for the Regiment*, 71; Kelly, "Holding Kentucky," 1: 387; Shaw, *History of the Tenth*, 138.
75. *OR*, vol. 7: 84, 87, 79; Daniel, *Days of Glory*, 52; McMurtry, "Zollicoffer," 308; Van Horne, *Army of the Cumberland*, 45; J. A. Vaughan, "Fighting Them Over: Zollicoffer's Death," *NT* (June 22, 1895): 3; Speed S. Fry, "General Fry's Story," *NT* (November 8, 1883): 5; Prokopowicz, *All for the Regiment*, 73; Nicholas, "Mill Springs," 61.
76. *OR*, vol. 7: 93, 79; Kelly, "Holding Kentucky," 1: 387, 388; Van Horne, *Army of the Cumberland*, 45; Tarrant, *Wild Riders*, 90; Myers, *Zollie Tree*, 95; Thomas quoted in Prokopowicz, *All for the Regiment*, 73; Daniel, *Days of Glory*, 52; Cleaves, *Rock of Chickamauga*, 97.

Chapter 5

77. "Camp at Mill Springs" Elmore letters, IHS; Perrin, *Kentucky*, 391; "The War in Kentucky," *NT*, 1.
78. *Early Life and Times in Boone County, Indiana* (Lebanon, IN: Harden and Spahr, 1887), 315.

79. Prokopowicz, *All for the Regiment*, 75, 211 n.39; R. R. Risley, "More About Zollicoffer's Death," *NT* (August 3, 1893): 3; Shaw, *History of the Tenth*, 127.
80. *OR*, vol. 7: 90; Miller testimony, Kise Court-Martial.
81. Miller testimony, Kise Court-Martial; *OR*, vol. 7: 90; Brents, *Patriots and Guerrillas*, 116; Shaw, *History of the Tenth*, 139.
82. "Camp at Mill Springs" Elmore letters, IHS; *OR*, vol. 7: 90; Kise also quoted in Williams, *Grant Rises*, 172; Perkins testimony, Kise Court-Martial; Nicholas, "Mill Springs," 60.
83. Brents, *Patriots and Guerrillas*, 116; Kelly, "Holding Kentucky," 1: 387; Perrin, *Kentucky*, 391; "War in Kentucky," *NT*, 1; Janet B. Hewett, ed., *Supplement to the Official Records of the Union and Confederate Armies* (Wilmington, NC: Broadfoot Publishing Company, 1996), Part 2, *Record of Events*, Volume 21, Serial No. 35: 683, 678; Tarrant, "Mill Springs," 4.
84. Tarrant, *Wild Riders*, 4.
85 Carroll testimony, Kise Court-Martial; Tarrant, *Wild Riders*, 90; "Camp at Mill Springs" Elmore letters, IHS; Shaw quoted in Prokopowicz, *All for the Regiment*, 71.
86. "Camp at Mill Springs," Elmore letters, IHS; "Dedication of Zollicoffer Monument," *CV*, 568; Derrick B. Harrison letter, IHS.
87. Tarrant, *Wild Riders*, 91, 96; Carroll testimony, Kise Court-Martial.
88. Gregory testimony, Kise Court-Martial; Maria Campbell Brent and Joseph E. Brent, *Interpretive Plan for the Mill Springs Battlefield* (Versailles, KY: Mudpuppy and Waterdog, 2011), 2: 11; *OR*, vol. 7: 86.
89. "Well my dear uncle and aunt" letter, January 23, 1862, Samuel Patterson Papers, IHS; "Camp at Mill Springs," Elmore letters, IHS; Shaw, *History of the Tenth*, 139, 153.
90. Johnston testimony, Miller testimony, Gregory testimony, Kise Court-Martial.
91. *OR*, vol. 70: 90–91; Miller testimony, Kise Court-Martial; McIlvaine and Elmore quoted in Prokopowicz, *All for the Regiment*, 73.
92. Gregory testimony, Miller testimony, Johnston testimony, Kise Court-Martial; William C. Kise, "The Tenth Indiana at Mill Springs," *NT* (November 8, 1883): 5; Derrick B. Harrison letter, IHS; Shaw, *History of the Tenth*, 151; Moore, ed., *Rebellion Record*, 4: 42; *OR*, vol. 7: 100; Tarrant, *Wild Riders*, 96.
93. Tarrant, *Wild Riders*, 96, 90; Miller testimony, Kise Court-Martial.
94. Gregory testimony, Kise Court-Martial; *OR*, vol. 7: 86.
95. Kise, "Tenth Indiana," 5; Miller testimony, Perkins testimony, Gregory testimony, Carroll testimony, Kise testimony, Kise Court-Martial; *OR*, vol.

7: 84, 86, 90; Shaw, "History of the Tenth," 139; "dear uncle and aunt" letter, Samuel Patterson Papers, IHS; Tarrant, "Mill Springs," 4; *New York Times*, "The Campaign in Kentucky," January 26, 1862.

96. *New York Times*, "The Battle of Mill Spring, Ky.: Part Taken by the Minnesota Second," February 16, 1862.

Chapter 6

97. Fry testimony, Kise Court-Martial; *OR*, vol. 7: 84, 87; Fry, "Fry's Story," 759.

98. Perrin, *Kentucky*, 759; Richard C. Brown, *A History of Danville and Boyle County, Kentucky, 1774–1992* (Danville: Bicentennial Books, 1992), 29; Calvin Morgan Fackler, *Early Days in Danville* (Louisville, KY: The Standard Printing Co., 1941), 92–93, 203–04; 205; Kentucky Adjutant General Office, *Report of the Adjutant General of the State of Kentucky, Mexican War Veterans* (Frankfort, KY: John D. Woods, 1889), 36, 40; Jefferson J. Polk, *Autobiography of Dr. J.J. Polk* (Louisville, KY: John P. Morton and Co., 1867), 77.

99. Brown, *History of Danville*, 29–31; Perrin, *Kentucky*, 759–60; *Goodhue Volunteer*, March 5, 1862.

100. Van Horne, *Army of the Cumberland*, 24, 16; Thomas Speed, R. M. Kelly and Alfred Pirtle, *The Union Regiments of Kentucky* (Louisville, KY: Courier-Journal Job Printing, 1897), 302–03; Brown, *History of Danville*, 30. A number of sources note that the 4th Kentucky went into battle with four hundred men, including, *OR*, vol. 7: 88; Fry testimony, Kise Court-Martial; McMurtry, "Zollicoffer," 308; Perrin, *Kentucky*, 391; "The War in Kentucky," *NT*, 1.

101. Nicholas, "Mill Springs," 60; Prichard, "Glory Denied," 10.

102. Prokopowicz, *All for the Regiment*, 73; Vaughan, "Fighting them Over," 3; Kise, "Tenth Indiana," 5; *OR*, vol. 7: 100; Daniel, *Days of Glory*, 52; McMurtry, "Zollicoffer," 308; Shaw, *History of the Tenth*, 139; Kelly, "Holding Kentucky," 1: 388; *OR*, 7: 84; Brents, *Patriots and Guerrillas*, 116.

103. Kelly, "Holding Kentucky," 1: 388; A. Neat, "Gen. Schoepf," *NT* (July 14, 1887): 3; *OR*, vol. 7: 91.

104. McMurray, *Twentieth Tennessee*, 350, 386–88; W. J. McMurray, "Tribune to Gen. J. A. Battle," *CV* 7 (February 1899): 78.

105. *OR* vol. 7: 87; Fry, "Fry's Story," 5; Vaughan, "Fighting them Over," 3.

106. Wright, "Zollicoffer," 496–97; Hurst, *Men of Fire*, 62; Walthall quoted in Nicholas, "Mill Springs," 60.
107. *OR*, vol. 7: 87; Kelly, "Holding Kentucky," 1: 388; Fry, "Fry's Story," 5; Vaughan, "Fighting them Over," 1.
108. Fry, "Fry's Story," 5.
109. Connelly, *Heartland*, 97–98; *St. Cloud Democrat*, February 6, 1862; *New York Times*, "The Campaign in Kentucky," January 26, 1862.
110. Kelly, "Holding Kentucky," 1: 388; Daniel, *Days of Glory*, 52; McMurtry, "Zollicoffer," 309; Myers, *Zollie Tree*, 96; *OR*, vol. 7: 87; *New York Times*, "The Campaign in Kentucky," January 26, 1862.
111. Wright, "Zollicoffer," 496–97; McMurray, *Twentieth Tennessee*, 123.
112. McMurray, *Twentieth Tennessee*, 200–01, 158, 122, 123, 434; Myers, *Zollie Tree*, 97; *OR*, vol. 7: 109; Head, *Campaigns and Battles of the Sixteenth Regiment*, 309; Fry, "Fry's Story," 5.
113. McMurray, *Twentieth Tennessee*, 123; *OR*, vol. 7: 88; *New York Times*, "The Rebels at the Battle of Mill Spring," February 9, 1862
114. *St. Cloud Democrat*, February 6, 1862; "trees were flecked" quoted in Bobrick, *Master of War*, 96.
115. Nicholas, "Mill Springs," 60; Wright, "Zollicoffer," 497; McMurray, *Twentieth Tennessee*, 201; Worsham, *Nineteenth Tennessee*, 22; Harrison B. York, *Record of the 9th Independent Battery, Ohio Veteran Volunteer Artillery* (Cleveland, OH: Fairbank, Benedict, and Co., 1864), 21; *OR*, vol. 7: 100, 108, 107, 94; McMurtry, "Zollicoffer," 310; Kelly, "Holding Kentucky," 1: 389; Moore, *Rebellion Record*, 42.
116. *OR*, vol. 7: 101, 80; Perrin, *Kentucky*, 391.
117. Cooper, "Service with the Twentieth," 16; Daniel, *Soldiering*, 41; McMurray, *Twentieth Tennessee*, 201, 390; Connelly, *Heartland*, 98; author's interview with Bill Neikirk, Mill Springs battlefield, March 9, 2013. Additional sources noting the flintlocks not firing include *OR*, vol. 7: 108, 104; Horn, *Army of Tennessee*, 69; Woodworth, *Davis and His Generals*, 68.
118. Worsham, *Nineteenth Tennessee*, 22; Hurst, *Men of Fire*, 64; Bell Irvine Wiley, *The Life of Johnny Reb: The Common Soldier of the Confederacy* (Baton Rouge: Louisiana State University, 1943), 288–89; Daniel, *Soldiering*, 42; Connelly, *Heartland*, 98; Davis, *Rise and Fall*, 2: 20–21; Hancock, *Hancock's Diary*, 124.
119. Davis, *Rise and Fall*, 2: 22; Wright, "Zollicoffer," 497; McMurray, *Twentieth Tennessee*, 124.

CHAPTER 7

120. Prichard, "Glory Denied," 10; McMurray, *Twentieth Tennessee*, 201; Nicholas, "Mill Spring," 62; *OR*, vol. 7: 107; Hurst, *Men of Fire*, 63; Worsham, *Nineteenth Tennessee*, 23; Cummings Battle Report transcript, MSBC; *Memphis Daily Appeal*, "Death of Gen. Zollicoffer," July 9, 1870.
121. Kelly, "Holding Kentucky," 1: 388; Prokopowicz, *All for the Regiment*, 74; *Memphis Daily Appeal*, "Death of General Zollicoffer," July 9, 1870; Brown, *History of Danville*, 30.
122. Fry, "Fry's Story," 5; Perrin, *Kentucky*, 393n; *Memphis Daily Appeal*, "Death of Gen. Zollicoffer," July 9, 1870; Vaughan, "Fighting Them Over," 3.
123. Wright, "Zollicoffer," 492; *Memphis Daily Appeal*, "Death of Gen. Zollicoffer," July 9, 1870; Kelly, "Holding Kentucky," 1: 388; Perrin, *Kentucky*, 393n; Fry, "Fry's Story," 5.
124. Fry, "Fry's Story," 5; Perrin, *Kentucky*, 393n; *Memphis Daily Appeal*, "Death of Gen. Zollicoffer," July 9, 1870; Kelly, "Holding Kentucky," 1: 388–89; Brown, *History of Danville*, 30; Prokopowicz, *All for the Regiment*, 74; Wright, "Zollicoffer," 492, 492n. "It's the enemy, general," from Harrison, *Civil War*, 26; Brown, *History of Danville*, 30. Tarrant relates that Zollicoffer rode up to Fry, yelling, "Cease firing there, those are the Mississippians!" Tarrant, *Wild Riders*, 96.
125. Perrin, *Kentucky*, 393n; Fry, "Fry's Story," 5; Vaughan, "Fighting Them Over," 3; *Memphis Daily Appeal*, "Death of Gen. Zollicoffer," July 9, 1870; Tarrant, *Wild Riders*, 96; Myers, *Zollie Tree*, ix; Fry testimony, Kise Court-Martial.
126. Myers, *Zollie Tree*, 122 n8; Vaughan, "Fighting Them Over," 3; Hurst, *Men of Fire*, 63; *OR*, vol. 7: 86; Tarrant, *Wild Riders*, 96; Wright, "Zollicoffer," 492; Kelly, "Holding Kentucky," 1: 389; *Memphis Daily Appeal*, "Death of Gen. Zollicoffer," July 9, 1870.
127. *OR*, vol. 7: 81; "Camp at Mill Springs," Wesley Elmore letters, IHS; John Dow to "Dear Ann," January 21, 1862, letter, Dow Family Papers, Correspondence 1862, MSS A D744 Z, Filson Historical Society, Louisville; Shaw, *History of the Tenth*, 139.
128. Shaw, *History of the Tenth*, 153; John C. Widdle, "Fighting Them Over: The 1st Ky. Cav.," *NT* (October 18, 1888): 3; "Information Asked and Given," *NT* (July 28, 1887): 3; *Columbia Herald* [TN], June 17, 1870; *Nashville Union and American*, June 7, 1870; *Mount Vernon Signal* [KY], February 23, 1900.
129. Brown, *History of Danville*, 30; Thomas Speed, *The Union Cause in Kentucky, 1860–1865* (New York: The Knickerbocker Press, 1907), 198;

I.B. Webster, "Gen. Zollicoffer's Death," *NT* (April 21, 1892): 4; Hall quoted in James R. Fleming, *Band of Brothers: Company C, 9th Tennessee Infantry* (Shippensburg, PA: White Mane Publishing, 1996), 37–38.

130. Jefferson J. Polk, *Autobiography of J.J. Polk* (Louisville, KY: John P. Morton and Co., 1867), 78; Brown, *History of Danville*, 31, *Louisville Journal* quoted, 31.

131. *Memphis Daily Appeal*, "Death of Gen. Zollicoffer," July 9, 1870; Richardson quoted in Head, *Campaigns and Battles*, 309 n.

132. Officer quoted in Wright, "Zollicoffer," 493; *Cleveland Morning Leader*, January 25, 1862.

133. Vaughan, "Fighting Them Over," 3.

134. "sent straightway" from Moore, *Rebellion Record*, 4: 45; and quoted in Horn, *Army of Tennessee*, 440; Thomas Corwin Potter, "Dear Sister" letter transcript, January 24, 1862, MSBC; Wright, "Zollicoffer," 497n; M. G. Reis, "Zollicoffer's Death," *NT* (October 12, 1893): 3; Vaughan, "Fighting Them Over," 3; Nicholas, "Mill Springs," 71.

135. Nicholas, "Mill Springs," 63; Tarrant, *Wild Riders*, 93, 96; Brown, *History of Danville*, 30.

136. Prokopowicz, *All for the Regiment*, 74, 75; Hurst, *Men of Fire*, 63; Prichard, "Glory Denied," 10; Nicholas, "Mill Springs," 63; Hancock, *Hancock's Diary*, 126; Harrison, *Civil War*, 26–27.

Chapter 8

137. Nicholas, "Mill Springs," 63; Mill Springs Battlefield Association, "Battle of Mill Springs," *Kentucky's Civil War*, 59; Moore, *Rebellion Record*, 4: 43; Shaw, *History of the Tenth*, 153.

138. Myers, *Zollie Tree*, 97, 98, 99; McMurtry, "Zollicoffer," 310; *OR*, vol. 7: 107; Nicholas, "Mill Springs," 63; McMurray, *Twentieth Tennessee*, 202; *Clarksville Chronicle* [TN], February 7, 1862.

139. *OR*, vol. 7: 112.

140. Ibid., 113; *New York Times*, "The Rebels at the Battle of Mill Spring," February 9, 1862; P. T. Martin, "Recollections of a Confederate," *CV* 15 (May 1907): 231; F.T. Gibson, "Reminiscences of the Seventeenth Tennessee Regiment," *CV* 2 (January 1894): 21.

141. *OR*, vol. 7: 113, 114.

142. W. Calvin Dickinson, "An Interrupted Life; Colonel Sidney Smith Stanton," in Kent T. Dollar, Larry H. Whiteaker and W. Calvin Dickinson,

eds., *Sister States, Enemy States* (Lexington: University Press of Kentucky, 2009), 291; McMurray, *Twentieth Tennessee*, 202; *OR*, vol. 7: 107.

143. *OR*, vol. 7: 112; 107.

144. Myers, *Zollie Tree*, 98; *OR*, vol. 7: 79, 80, 87, 84; Thomas testimony, Kise Court-Martial; "War in Kentucky," *NT*, 1.

145. Nicholas, "Mill Springs," 64; Myers, *Zollie Tree*, 100; Prokopowicz, *All for the Regiment*, 76; Tarrant, *Wild Riders*, 91; Daniel, *Days of Glory*, 53; Van Horne, *Army of the Cumberland*, 45; Kelly, "Holding Kentucky," 1: 389.

146. *OR*, vol. 7: 93; Prokopowicz, *All for the Regiment*, 76; *OR*, vol. 7: 84, 96; Daniel, *Days of Glory*, 53; Bishop, *Minnesota*, 83; Kelly, "Holding Kentucky," 1: 389.

147. *OR*, 7: 93, 80.

148. Van Cleve testimony, Kise Court-Martial; *Goodhue Volunteer*, March 5, 1862; *New York Times*, "Minnesota Second," February 16, 1862; Fitch, *Annals*, 174; Bishop, *Minnesota*, 79; H. M. Bayless, "Mill Springs," *NT* (May 5, 1887): 3; *OR*, vol. 7: 93, 95; Chester, *Drummer Boy's Diary*, 13.

149. *OR*, vol. 7: 93; Binford quoted in Nicholas, "Mill Springs," 64.

150. Bishop, *Minnesota*, 84; George testimony, McCook testimony, Van Cleve testimony, Kise Court-Martial; *OR*, vol. 7: 93, 80; Shaw, *History of the Tenth*, 139; Fry, "Fry's Story," 5.

151. Jennison testimony, George testimony, Fry testimony, Kise Court-Martial.

152. Kelly, "Holding Kentucky," 1: 389; Bishop, *Minnesota*, 83; *New York Times*, "Minnesota Second," February 16, 1862; S.P. Jennison, "The Illustrations of a Soldier" in *Glimpses of the Nation's Struggle: A Series of Papers Read Before the Minnesota Commandery of the Military Order of the Loyal Legion of the United States* (St. Paul, MN: St. Paul Book and Stationary Co., 1887): 377; *Goodhue Volunteer*, March 5, 1862; *OR*, vol. 7: 95, 93; Bishop, *Minnesota*, 84; Strong quoted in Edward Duffield Neill, *The History of Minnesota* (Minneapolis, MN: Johnson, Smith and Harrison, 1878), 686n.

153. Prokopowicz, *All for the Regiment*, 77; Chester, *Drummer Boy's Diary*, 13; Harrison, *Civil War*, 27; *New York Times*, "Minnesota Second," February 16, 1862; Van Cleve and Parker quoted in Nicholas, "Mill Springs," 64–65; Edward Duffield Neill, *The History of Minnesota* (Minneapolis, MN: Johnson, Smith, and Harrison, 1878), 686n.

154. Tarrant, *Wild Riders*, 91; *OR*, vol. 7: 94, 83; Frank Moore and Thomas Commerford Martin, *Reminiscences of Pioneer Days in St. Paul* (N.p.: Kissinger Publishing, 2004 [1908]), 79.

155. McMurray, *Twentieth Tennessee*, 75, 76; Bishop, *Minnesota*, 84; Moore and Martin, *Pioneer Days*, 80; Cleaves, *Rock of Chickamauga*, 98, 100; *Cincinnati Daily Press*, February 4, 1862; Welles quoted in Neill, *History of Minnesota*, 686n.

CHAPTER 9

156. *OR*, vol. 7: 96; Don Heinrich Tolzmann, trans., Gustav Tafel, *The Cincinnati Germans in the Civil War* (Milford, OH: Little Miami Publishing Co., 2010), 28, 29; "War in Kentucky," *NT*, 1; David Bittle Floyd, *History of the Seventy-fifth Regiment of Indiana Infantry Volunteers* (Philadelphia: Lutheran Publication Society, 1893), 212; Charles Whalen and Barbara Whalen, *The Fighting McCooks: America's Famous Fighting Family* (Bethesda, MD: Westmoreland Press, 2006), 98; *Lafayette Courier* quoted in the *Cincinnati Daily Press*, January 27, 1862.
157. Whalen and Whalen, *Fighting McCooks*, 98, 99, 105; Talzmann, *Cincinnati Germans*, 27, 32; Floyd, *Seventy-fifth Regiment*, 213; Frederic Trautman, trans., Constantin Grebner, *We Were the Ninth: A History of the Ninth Regiment, Ohio Volunteer Infantry, April 17, 1861, to June 7, 1864* (Kent, OH: Kent State University Press), 81, 82; Whitelaw Reid, *Ohio in the War; Her Statesmen, Her Generals, and Soldiers* (Cincinnati, OH: Moore, Wilstach and Baldwin, 1868), 2: 72–73; *OR*, vol. 7: 80.
158. *OR*, vol. 7: 96; Hurst, *Men of Fire*, 63; Kelly, "Holding Kentucky," 1: 389; Prokopowicz, *All for the Regiment*, 79.
159. *OR*, vol. 7: 96, 94, 93; Prokopowicz, *All for the Regiment*, 76, 77; *St. Cloud Democrat*, February 6, 1862; Nicholas, "Mill Springs," 66; Myers, *Zollie Tree*, 99.
160. *OR*, vol. 7: 96, 94, 77, 81; Whalen and Whalen, *Fighting McCooks*, 106; Neat, "Schoepf," 3; *Local News* [Alexandria, VA], January 23, 1862.
161. Trautman, *We Were the Ninth*, 83; Brent and Brent, *Interpretive Plan*, 2: 95; Reid, *Ohio in the War*, 2: 201; *OR*, vol. 7: 94.
162. Perkins testimony, Miller testimony, Carroll testimony, Kise Court-Martial; Kise, "Tenth Indiana," 5; Shaw, *Tenth Regiment*, 139; Van Horne, *Army of the Cumberland*, 45; *OR*, vol. 7: 91.
163. Johnston testimony, Miller testimony, Carroll testimony, Perkins testimony, Kise Court-Martial; Kise, "Tenth Indiana," 5; *OR*, vol. 7: 91.
164. Johnston testimony, Miller testimony, Kise Court-Martial; Kise, "Tenth Indiana," 5.
165. Hurst, *Men of Fire*, 64; William J. Kaan, "Mahlon D. Manson and the Civil War in Kentucky: The Politics of Martial Glory," *Register of the Kentucky Historical Society* 96 (Summer 1998): 234; *OR*, vol. 7: 97; Williams, *Grant Rises*, 174; Prokopowicz, *All for the Regiment*, 76.
166. *OR*, vol. 7: 97, 98; Wright, "Zollicoffer," 497; Kelly, "Holding Kentucky," 1: 389; Mill Springs Battlefield Association, "Battle of Mill Springs," 59; Perrin, *Kentucky*, 391; "War in Kentucky," *NT*, 1; W. Wallace, "Cumberland Gap," *NT* (July 26, 1906): 6; Daniel, *Days of Glory*, 53; Fitch, *Annals*, 62; Tarrant, *Wild Riders*, 91.

167. *OR*, vol. 7: 97, 98.
168. Ibid., 94.
169. Ibid., 94, 96; Whalen and Whalen, *Fighting McCooks*, 106, McCook quoted, 97; Trautman, *We Were the Ninth*, 84; Tolzmann, *Cincinnati Germans*, 35.
170. *OR*, vol. 7: 80, 96, 94; Trautman, *We Were the Ninth*, 83.
171. *New York Times*, "Minnesota Second," February 16, 1862; *Chicago Tribune*, "The Late Somerset Battle," January 29, 1862; Tarrant, *Wild Riders*, 97; Boynton quoted in Trautman, *We Were the Ninth*, 87.
172. Tarrant, *Wild Riders*, 91; *OR*, vol. 7: 107; Worsham, *Nineteenth Tennessee*, 23.
173. *OR*, vol. 7: 80, 94; Trautman, *We Were the Ninth*, 84.
174. Johnston testimony, Kise Court-Martial.
175. *OR*, vol. 7: 85, 91; Kise, "Tenth Indiana," 5; Miller testimony, Perkins testimony, Johnston testimony, Kise Court-Martial; *OR*, vol. 7: 91.
176. Stafford testimony, Kise Court-Martial; *OR*, vol. 7: 91, Kise, "Tenth Indiana," 5.
177. "Report of Maj. Horace Rice, Comdg 29th Tenn. Regt," Confederate States Army Casualties, Lists and Narrative Reports, 1861–1865, National Archives and Records Administration, Record Group 109, www.fold3 (accessed June 26, 2012); *OR*, vol. 7: 108, 113, 115; Nicholas, "Mill Springs," 68. *Memphis Daily Appeal*, January 28, 1862.
178. *OR*, vol. 7: 91; Shaw, *History of the Tenth*, 151; Derrick B. Harrison letter, IHS; Johnston testimony, Miller testimony, Kise Court-Martial; Kise, "Tenth Indiana," 5.
179. McCook testimony, Kise testimony, Fry testimony, Van Cleve testimony, Kise Court-Martial.

Chapter 10

180. Kelly, "Holding Kentucky," 1: 392.
181. Thomas testimony, George testimony, Kise Court-Martial; Brents, *Patriots and Guerrillas*, 116.
182. Tarrant, *Wild Riders*, 91; Daniel, *Days of Glory*, 53; Van Horne, *Army of the Cumberland*, 46; *OR*, vol. 7: 87–88, 108; McCook testimony, Kise Court-Martial; Thomas J. Stephenson to grandfather, January 26, 1862, letter, Civil War Letters of Joseph Guillion and Thomas J. Stephenson, Joseph Guillion Letters, SC662, IHS.
183. Worsham quoted in Hurst, *Men of Fire*, 65.

184. *OR*, vol. 7: 103, 104, 88, 89; "Dear Sister" letter, January 28, 1862, Dow family Papers, Correspondence 1862, Filson Historical Society; Prichard, "Glory Denied," 10; Fry, "Fry's Story," 5; Webster, "Zollicoffer's Death," 4; Speed, *Union Cause*, 197; Myers, *Zollie Tree*, 104; Marian F. Finn, "Picket Shots: Mill Springs," *NT* (July 18, 1895): 3; Tapp and Klotter, *John W. Tuttle*, 70. Harlan quoted in Speed, *Union Cause*, 197.
185. *OR*, vol. 7: 80, 91, 85; Nicholas, "Mill Springs," 68; Kelly, "Holding Kentucky," 1: 390; Jennison, "Illustrations," 379; "wildest confusion" from *Richmond Daily Dispatch*, January 25, 1862; Potter, "Dear Sister" letter, MSBA; Cassius M. Clay, "Postscript to the Battle of Mill Springs, *Filson Club History Quarterly* 30 (April 1956): 109; Berry, *Voices*, 280; "Major Henry G. Davidson," *American Phrenological Journal* (March 1865): 92; Wood quoted in Eubank, *Patriarch*, 64.
186. *OR*, vol. 7: 92, 94, 97, 80, 85, 114, 101; Harlan quoted in Beth, *Harlan*, 56; Williams, *Grant Rises*, 175; Kelly, "Holding Kentucky," 1: 390; Harrison, *Civil War*, 27; Myers, *Zollie Tree*, 106; Daniel, *Days of Glory*, 53; Potter, "Dear Sister" letter, MSBA; Mill Springs Battlefield Association, "Battle of Mill Springs," 59; Berry, *Voices*, 280.
187. *OR*, vol. 7: 109, 105, 114; Harrison, *Civil War*, 27; Crittenden quoted in Davis, *Rise and Fall*, 2: 21; *New York Times*, "The Rebel Retreat from Mill Spring," March 2, 1862; Mill Springs Battlefield Association, "Battle of Mill Springs," 59; Berry, *Voices*, 280; Dalton, "Zollicoffer," 469.
188. Fry quoted in Daniel, *Days of Glory*, 53; Worsham, *Nineteenth Tennessee*, 27.
189. York, *Record of the 9th Independent Battery*, 20, 22; *OR*, vol. 7: 97, 81; *New York Times*, "Rebel Retreat," March 2, 1862; "Well my dear uncle" letter, January 23, 1863 [1862], Samuel Patterson Papers, IHS; Dow to "Dear Sister," January 28, 1862, Dow family Papers, Filson Historical Society; "Camp at Mill Springs" letter, January 23, 1862, Elmore letters, IHS; Williams, *Grant Rises*, 175; Myers, *Zollie Tree*, 107; Tarrant, *Wild Riders*, 92; Daniel, *Days of Glory*, 54; Van Horne, *Army of the Cumberland*, 46.
190. Fry, "Fry's Story," 5; *Chicago Tribune*, "The Defeat of Zollicoffer," February 4, 1862; "Well my dear uncle," Patterson Papers, IHS; *New York Times*, "Affairs in Kentucky," February 6, 1862; Harrison, *Civil War*, 27; Shaw, *Tenth Regiment*, 139; Derrick B. Harrison letter, IHS.
191. Speed, *Union Cause*, 198; Berry, *Voices*, 280; *OR*, vol. 7: 81, 85, 89; Shaw, *Tenth Regiment*, 153; Speed, *Union Regiments*, 368; Harlan quoted in Beth, *Harlan*, 56; "Dear Ann" letter, January 21, 1862, Dow Family Papers, Filson Historical Society; "Camp at Mill Springs" letter, January 23, 1862.

192. Moore, *Rebellion Record*, 4: 44; Thompson, *Memoranda of James L. Hickerson*, 4; *OR*, vol. 7: 85; Thomas quoted in Kelly, "Holding Kentucky," 1: 391; McMurtry, "Zollicoffer," 311.
193. "Dear Uncle" letter, January 23, 1863 [1862], Samuel Patterson Papers, IHS; Henry Howe, *The Times of the Rebellion in the West* (Cincinnati, OH: Howe's Subscription Book Concern, 1867), 98; *OR*, vol. 7: 76, 86; "Dear Ann" letter, January 21, 1862, "Dear Sister" letter, January 28, 1862, Dow Family Papers, Filson Historical Society; Shaw, *Tenth Regiment*, 153; Kelly, "Holding Kentucky," 1: 390–91; Berry, *Voices*, 280; Chester, *Drummer Boy's Diary*, 13; Webster, "Zollicoffer's Death," 4; Derrick B. Harrison letter, IHS; Wallace, "Cumberland Gap," 6; Williams, *Grant Rises*, 175; Moore, *Rebellion Record*, "Poetry and Incidents," 4: 75; *Cleveland Morning Leader*, January 23, 1862; January 25, 1862; *Catalogue of the Museum of Flags, Trophies and Relics, Relating to the Revolution, the War of 1812, the Mexican War, and the Present Rebellion; Forming the Most Complete and Interesting Collection ever Brought Together in the United States: To Be Exhibited at New York, April 4, 1864* (New York: Charles O. Jones, 1864), 74; *New York Times*, "The Rebels at the Battle of Mill Spring," February 9, 1862; *New York Times*, "Affairs in Kentucky," February 6, 1862; Clay, "Postscript," 109; "Camp at Mill Springs" letter, January 23, 1862, Elmore letters, IHS; *Cincinnati Daily Press*, February 3, 1862.
194. *New York Times*, "The Rebels at the Battle of Mill Spring," February 9, 1862; "Dear Sister" letter, January 28, 1862, "Dear Sister" letter, January 21, 1862; Dow Family Correspondence, 1862, Filson Historical Society.
195. Moore, *Rebellion Record*, 4: 44; F.M. Aldridge to "Dear Lizzie," January 30, 1862, Francis Marion Aldridge Papers, MS21755, Series 1, Box 1, Folder 8, Mississippi Department of Archives and History, transcription in MSBC; *New York Times*, "The Campaign in Kentucky," January 26, 1862.
196. *White Cloud Kansas Chief*, May 15, 1862; *National Republican*, February 13, 1862.
197. *Clarksville* [TN] *Chronicle*, August 12, 1870.
198. Kelly, "Holding Kentucky," 1: 390; *OR*, vol. 7: 83; Thompson, *Memoranda of James L. Hickerson*, 4; Nicholas, "Mill Springs," 71; Speed, *Union Regiments*, 474.
199. *OR*, vol. 7: 81, 563, 564; Clay, "Postscript," 109, 110; Berry, *Voices*, 280.
200. *OR*, vol. 7: 103, 114, 875, 103, 110.
201. *New York Times*, "Letter from Col. Fry," February 3, 1862; *Chicago Tribune*, "The Defeat of Zollicoffer," February 4, 1862; Eubank, *Patriarch*, 64; *OR*, vol. 7: 110; Myers, *Zollie Tree*, 181; Dickinson, "Stanton," 291.

202. Nicholas, "Mill Springs," 71; *OR*, vol. 7: 930; Daniel, *Days of Glory*, 54–55.
203. Moore, *Rebellion Record*, "Poetry and Incidents," 4: 75.
204. Webster, "Zollicoffer's Death," 4; F.W. Keil, *Thirty-fifth Ohio: A Narrative of Service from August, 1861 to 1864* (Fort Wayne, IN: Archer, Housh, and Co., 1894), 37.
205. Tarrant, *Wild Riders*, 99, 96.
206. E. J., "A Ride to the Battle," *Cleveland Daily Herald*, January 28, 1862; *Cincinnati Daily Press*, January 24, 1862; February 8, 1862; January 25, 1862; Derrick B. Harrison letter, IHS; *New York Times*, "The Campaign in Kentucky," January 26, 1862; *Chicago Tribune*, "The Late Somerset Battle," January 29, 1862.
207. "Dedication of Zollicoffer Monument," *CV*, 574; *Memphis Daily Appeal*, "Death of Gen. Zollicoffer," July 9, 1870; Fry, "Fry's Story," 5; Vaughan, "Fighting Them Over," 3; *Cincinnati Daily Press*, February 11, 1862.
208. E. J., "Ride to the Battle"; Neill, *History of Minnesota*, 686n; Speed, *Union Cause*, 197; James L. Cooper, "Sketches of War and Prison Life," *CV* 15 (December 1907): 547.
209. Myers, *Zollie Tree*, 126–27, 181; *Cincinnati Daily Press*, January 23, 1862; Manson quoted in *Richmond Daily Dispatch*, February 8, 1862; Thompson, *Memoranda of James L. Hickerson*, 5; Small diary, IHS; *OR*, vol. 7: 565; Hancock, *Hancock's Diary*, 125; *Memphis Daily Appeal*, "Death of Gen. Zollicoffer," July 9, 1870; Woodruff, "Zollicoffer's Death," 3.
210. Myers, *Zollie Tree*, 128; Liberty Warner to "Dear Friends," an "Early Jan. 1862" letter, Liberty Warner Papers, Transcripts-M5624, Bowling Green State University, Bowling Green, OH, www.bgsu.edu/colleges/library/cac/ms/trans/page53869.html (accessed October 1, 2011); *Cincinnati Daily Press*, January 31, 1862; Cyrus Reasoner to wife Lizza, Camp Wood, Hart County, Kentucky, January 30, 1862, Cyrus Reasoner Civil War Correspondence, Northern Kentucky University, http://archives.nku.edu/special_collections/collections/reasoner/index/php (accessed October 18, 2011); *Semi-Weekly Shreveport News*, March 4, 1862.
211. *New York Times*, "A Flag of Truce," February 6, 1862; Kathy Lauder, ed. "Diary of John Berrien Lindsley, 1861-1865, ABRIDGED," Tennessee State Library and Archives, www.tennessee.gov/tsla/.../lindsley%20diary%201861-1865.doc (accessed December 13, 2012); McMurtry, "Zollicoffer," 314.
212. *St. Cloud Democrat*, February 6, 1862; "Dear Ann" letter, Dow Family Papers, Correspondence 1862, Filson Historical Society; Keil, *Thirty-fifth Ohio*, 41–42.

213. E. J., "Ride to the Battle."

214. Myers, *Zollie Tree*, 111; *OR*, vol. 7: 81; Brent and Brent, *Interpretive Plan*, 2: 61; *Fremont Journal* [Ohio], "Incidents of Mill Springs," January 31, 1862; *Cincinnati Daily Press*, January 25, 1862; Bennett H. Young, "Battle of Fishing Creek—'Zollie Tree,'" *CV* 19 (March 1911): 110; "From Tablet Near Zollicoffer Monument in Kentucky," *CV* 19 (February 1911): 73.

215. Keil, *Thirty-fifth Ohio*, 42.

216. Dr. J.S. Newberry, *The U.S. Sanitary Commission in the Valley of the Mississippi* (Cleveland, OH: Fairbank, Benedict, and Co., 1871), 304; Joseph K. Barnes, *The Medical and Surgical History of the War of the Rebellion* (Wilmington, NC: Broadfoot Publishing, 1990), 2: 23, 24; *Chicago Tribune*, "No Ambulances," February 7, 1862; *New York Times*, "The Rebels at the Battle of Mill Springs," February 9, 1862; Worsham, *Nineteenth Tennessee*, 23; Clay, "Postscript," 110; *Richmond Daily Dispatch*, February 8, 1862; *Clarksville Chronicle*, January 31, 1862.

217. Cooper, "Service," 16; Barnes, *Surgical History*, 2: 24.

218. *OR*, vol. 7: 76, 78; Williams, *Grant Rises*, 175; Mill Springs Battlefield Association, "Battle of Mill Springs," 59; Harrison and Klotter, *New History*, 197; Eubank, *Patriarch*, 63; Nicholas, "Mill Springs," 71.

219. *OR*, vol. 7; 82, 100, 92, 86, 95, 108; Shaw, *Tenth Regiment*, 144; Tarrant, *Wild Riders*, 94; Perrin, *Kentucky*, 392; Speed, *Union Regiments*, 306; *New York Times*, "Minnesota Second," February 16, 1862; Van Cleve testimony, Kise Court-Martial.

220. *New York Times*, "Rebels at the Battle," February 9, 1862; Kelly, "Holding Kentucky," 1: 392, 390; *OR*, vol. 7: 108, 114; Rowland, *Statistical Register*, 617; Wright, "Zollicoffer," 498; Myers, *Zollie Tree*, 101; Cummings Battle Report, MSBC; McMurray, *Twentieth Tennessee*, 390; Hurst, *Men of Fire*, 64.

221. *OR*, vol. 7: 108, 115; Rice report, NARA, via Fold3.

222. *OR*, vol. 7: 108; Hurst, *Men of Fire*, 64.

223. Prichard, "Glory Denied," 11; Fitch, *Annals*, 63; *OR*, vol. 7: 568, 589, 582; Myers, *Zollie Tree*, 117.

CHAPTER 11

224. *OR*, vol. 7: 102; Clay, "Postscript," 108; "Dear Ann" letter, January 21, 1862, Correspondence 1862, Dow Family Papers, Filson Historical Society; "Davidson," *American Phrenological Journal*, 92; *Vermont Phoenix*,

January 23, 1862; *New York Times*, "The Battle of Mill Spring," January 25, 1862; *Cincinnati Daily Press*, January 21, 1862; *Chicago Tribune*, "Reaction in England," March 1, 1862.

225. Worsham, *Nineteenth Tennessee*, 26; Prichard, "Glory Denied," 11; Larry J. Daniel, *Shiloh: The Battle that Changed the Civil War* (New York: Simon and Schuster, 1997), 21, 22, *Charleston Mercury* quoted, 22; *OR*, vol. 7: 849, 850; Hancock, *Hancock's Diary*, 124; Crittenden quoted in Davis, *Rise and Fall*, 2: 21; *New York Times*, "The Defeat at Somerset," February 9, 1862; Eubank, *Patriarch*, 64; *Chicago Tribune*, "Late Southern News," February 6, 1862; Coleman, *John J. Crittenden*, 2: 347; *OR*, vol. 7: 850, 855,871–72, 379.

226. Myers, *Zollie Tree*, 181–82; Nicholas, "Mill Springs," 72.

227. Speed, *Union Cause*, 194.

228. Tarrant, *Wild Riders*, 84.

229. Myers, "Who Owns," 239; *Acts of the General Assembly of the Commonwealth of Kentucky* [1879–1880 session] (Frankfort: Kentucky Yeoman, 1880), 2: 164–65; "List of National Cemeteries, Showing the Number of Internments in each, June 30, 1893," *NT* (February 8, 1894): 7.

230. Myers, "Who Owns," 239, 240; Young, "Battle of Fishing Creek," 110; "Dedication of Zollicoffer Monument," *CV*, 567, 568; Myers, *Zollie Tree*, 4.

231. Myers, "Who Owns," 240, 241, 242.

232. Brent and Brent, *Interpretive Plan*, 1: 2, i; Myers, *Zollie Tree*, 1, xxii; "Rogers Introduces Legislation to Honor and Preserve Mill Springs Battlefield," press release from http://halrogers.house.gov/news/documentsingle.aspx?DocumentID=316994 (accessed April 13, 2013).

A Note on Sources

Because of the detailed endnotes, an exhaustive bibliography has not been included. Several key sources, however, have been essential. First, the files of the Mill Springs Battlefield Association provided information about the battle and efforts to commemorate the site. Another critical source was volume 7 of the U.S. War Department's *The War of the Rebellion: A Compilation of the Official Records of the Union and Confederate Armies* (1880–1901), which includes correspondence and reports about the campaign and battle.

Mark D. Jaeger kindly provided his transcript of Kise's court-martial proceeding from the National Archives in Washington, D.C. Containing the testimony of officers and soldiers, this source was crucial. The collections of the Indiana Historical Society were also extremely important, as were the Dow Family Papers at the Filson Historical Society and several collections from the Kentucky Historical Society.

Beneficial regimental histories included R. R. Hancock's *Hancock's Diary, Or, A History of the Second Tennessee Confederate Cavalry* (1887); W. J. McMurray's *History of the Twentieth Tennessee Regiment Volunteer Infantry, CSA* (1904); W. J. Worsham's *The Old Nineteenth Tennessee Regiment, CSA* (1902); J. A. Brents' *The Patriots and Guerrillas of East Tennessee and Kentucky* (1863); Constantin Grebner's *We Were the Ninth: A History of the Ninth Regiment, Ohio Volunteer Infantry, April 17, 1861, to June 7, 1864*; F. W. Keil's *Thirty-fifth Ohio: A Narrative of Service from August, 1861 to 1864* (1894); James Birney Shaw's *History of the Tenth Regiment, Indiana Volunteer Infantry* (1912); and Eastham Tarrant's *The Wild Riders of the 1st Kentucky Cavalry* (1894). R. M. Kelly's "Holding Kentucky for the Union," from *Battles and Leaders of the Civil War*, is a solid overview. The letters of Union soldier Green Clay, published in Mary Clay Berry's *Voices from the Century Before: The Odyssey of a 19th Century Kentucky Family*, and Cassius M. Clay's "Postscript to the Battle of Mill Springs," which appeared in the *Filson Club History Quarterly* (1956), were also illuminating.

The postwar recollections of soldiers that appeared in *Confederate Veteran*, *National Tribune* and period newspapers were also useful. As the reputed slayer of Zollicoffer, Fry gave several newspaper interviews about his role and published his own version of the event. Many soldiers also commented on the shooting and the plundering of Zollicoffer's corpse.

For those interested in further reading, Raymond E. Myers's *The Zollie Tree: General Felix K. Zollicoffer and the Battle of Mill Springs*, provides an account of Zollicoffer's life, while Kenneth A. Hafendorfer's *Mill Springs: Campaign and Battle of Mill Springs, Kentucky*, is a detailed account of the campaign and battle. Other secondary sources listed in the endnotes provide overviews of the armies and campaign.

Although not reflected in the endnotes, an extensive battlefield tour led by Bill Neikirk, former president of the Mill Springs Battlefield Association, greatly aided my comprehension of the fight. For additional sources, please consult the endnotes. For a greater understanding of the battle, please visit the Mill Springs battlefield.

Index

D

E

F

G

H

U

V

W

Y

Z

About the Author

Stuart W. Sanders is former executive director of the Perryville Battlefield Preservation Association. He is author of *Perryville Under Fire: The Aftermath of Kentucky's Largest Civil War Battle* (The History Press, 2012) and has contributed to the books *Kentuckians in Gray: Confederate Generals and Field Officers of the Bluegrass State*, *Confederate Generals in the Western Theater* (volumes II and III) and *Confederate Generals of the Trans-Mississippi* (volumes I and II, forthcoming). Sanders has written for *Civil War Times Illustrated*, *America's Civil War*, *Military History Quarterly*, *Hallowed Ground*, *Kentucky Humanities*, the *Journal of America's Military Past*, *Kentucky Ancestors*, the *Register of the Kentucky Historical Society*, *Blue and Gray*, *Encyclopedia Virginia* and several other publications. He is currently a public history administrator in the Commonwealth of Kentucky.